AF364427

Basics of SIMULINK for Engineers

Basics of SIMULINK for Engineers

Dr. Pillarisetty Anil Kumar
Scientist – G,
Research Center Imarat (RCI), DRDO,
Hyderabad-69

Dr. G. Janardhana Raju
Dean, School of Engineering
Professor of Mechanical Engineering
Nalla Narasimha Reddy Education Society's Group of Institutions,
Hyderabad-88

BS Publications
An Imprint of BSP Books Pvt. Ltd.
4-4-309/316, Giriraj Lane, Sultan Bazar,
Hyderabad - 500 095.

Published by:

BSP BS Publications

An Imprint of BSP Books Pvt., Ltd.

4-4-309/316, Giriraj Lane, Sultan Bazar,

Hyderabad - 500 095

Phone : 040 - 23445688

e-mail : info@bspbooks.net

Website : www.bspbooks.net

ISBN: 978-93-95038-05-8 (Hardback)

I wish to dedicate this book to my cute daughter Baby Pillarisetty Kamaneeya and my beloved wife Dr. Mukkamalla Viswajyothi and offer this work at the lotus feet of the Universal Spirit.

Dr. Pillarisetty Anil Kumar

I wish to dedicate this book to my parents Sri G. Vengama Raju and Smt. G. Reddemma; my wife Dr. P. A. Harsha Vardhini, and my children G. Sai Krishiv Raju and G. Jasritha Sai.

Dr. Gangaraju Janardhana Raju

Acknowledgements

I express my deep sense of gratitude for the motivation and encouragement extended by Dr. P. Anil Kumar, Scientist –G, and Director, management Services, RCI, Hyderabad & Author of this book.

I am always thankful to Sri Nalla Narasimha Reddy, Chairman, Mr. Prashanth Reddy, Vice Chairman, Dr. C. V. Krishna Reddy, Director, Nalla Narasimha Reddy Education Society's Group of Institutions, Hyderabad for their constant encouragement during the course of work.

My heartfelt thanks to my mentors and research supervisors Dr. G. Ranga Janardhana, Professor of Mechanical Engineering and Vice Chancellor of JNTU Ananthapuramu, Andhra Pradesh and Dr. C. Subba Rao, Director, St. Ann's Engineering College, Cheerala, Andhra Pradesh for their continuous guidance.

I thank Dr. G. Hema Chandra Reddy, Chairman APSCHE and Dr. B. Sudheer Prem Kumar, Professor of Mechanical Engineering, JNTUH for their constant support.

I thank Mr. E. Vijaya Kumar, Director, VIMP Institute, Kadapa, Andhra Pradesh for his help during the compilation of the book.

I thank all my fellow Deans, HoDs, Faculty members of various schools and departments of Nalla Narasimha Reddy Group of Institutions for their continuous support and encouragement.

Last but not least, I thank my parents, Sri. G. Vengama Raju and Smt. G. Reddemma for their constant blessings throughout my career and development. My heartfelt thanks to my wife Dr. P.A. Harsha Vardhini for her support and encouragement. Special thanks to my children Sai Krishiv Raju and Jasritha Sai for their cooperation and patience.

Finally I thank all who have directly or indirectly supported me in completing this task.

-Authors

Preface

This book is exclusively planned for engineering students from all disciplines viz mechanical, electrical, electronics, etc. Contents of this book are framed in such a way that it becomes gateway for those who are interested to use Simulink. Capabilities of Simulink at elementary level are very well compiled. Total book comprises of nine chapters starting from introduction. Elementary level aspects like basic mathematical operations, matrices, algebraic equations, complex numbers, interpolation and extrapolation of data, etc are covered. Apart from these higher order aspects like calculus, plotting different signals, solving differential equations are also given due importance. Syllabus for BTech level subject can be framed based on the contents of this book. Simulink software offers Graphical User Interface (GUI) based platform where all functions are framed in form of blocks. For all the models details of blocks are elaborated to a greater extent. Idea behind writing this book is to enable the engineering students to learn Simulink software on self-study mode. Details are elaborated to minute level so that the reader can practice on his own. Problems of simple variety are chozen as worked out examples to entrust comfort to reader. All these endeavors are put forwarded to inculcate zeal in reader so that he/she can make best use of this book. Once the students practice all worked out problems in this book they will be competent enough to develop Simulink models for any advanced application oriented problems from any discipline.

-Authors

Contents

CHAPTER 9: SOLVING DIFFERENTIAL EQUATIONS

About the Authors

Dr. P. Anil Kumar has acquired his B.Tech (Mechanical Engineering) degree from JNTU, Hyderabad with first class with distinction in the year 1998. He joined in Defence R&D Organization (DRDO) in the year 2000. He started his career as Scientist 'B' in the area of structural dynamic analysis of sub systems and systems of air borne vehicles using finite element method. He has provided solutions for vibration problems in various electronic packages used in air borne vehicles. Unique solution provided by him for vibration problem in one of the vehicle interface unit gave sigh of relief for 150 units. From the wide spectrum of solutions provided he has formulated guidelines for structural design of electronic packages and circulated among electronic designers of his laboratory. He has vast experience in conducting ground resonance testing of full scale air borne vehicle, structural load testing and modal testing. He has received lab technology group award in the year 2008, lab scientist of the year award for the year 2010, Agni group award for excellence in self-reliance for the year 2014, Agni group award for excellence in self-reliance for the year 2016, DRDO group award for performance excellence for the year 2016 and RCI technology group award for the year 2018. He has 15 publications out of which two are related to the present work and one patent related to the present work. Presently he is editorial board member for International Journal of Mechanical Engineering and Applications (IJMEA). He did his Ph.D. on "Design and Development of Metallic Vibration Isolators for Air Borne Vehicles" from NIT, Warangal in the year 2018 under the guidance of Prof. P. Bangaru Babu.

Dr. G. Janardhana Raju is currently working as Dean, School of Engineering and Professor of Mechanical Engineering at Nalla Narasimha Reddy Education Society's Group of Institutions, Hyderabad, Telangana, India. He has published 75 papers in National and International peer reviewed reputed journals. Areas of interest of Dr.Raju are Industrial Engineering, Optimization Techniques, and Entrepreneurship Development. He is the co-investigator for one of the JNTUH/TEQIP-III, Govt. of India sponsored project. Under his supervision two scholars have been awarded Ph.D. and currently one scholar is pursuing his Ph.D. Apart from regular Mechanical Engineering subjects he has also taught the subjects like Computer Programming, Computer Simulation through MATLAB and SIMULINK for UG and PG Students.

Dr. G. J. Raju has completed his graduation (B.Tech) in Mechanical Engineering from KSRM College of Engineering, Kadapa, Andhra Pradesh in 1996 and M.Tech. in Industrial Engineering from Sri Venkateswara University, Tirupati, Andhra Pradesh in 1999. He has done his Ph.D. in Industrial Engineering from Jawaharlal Technological University Hyderabad, Andhra Pradesh in 2006.

He has total 22 years of teaching & administration experience and served teaching profession in various positions as Asst. Professor, Assoc. Professor, Professor, HoD, and Dean at different institutions *viz* KSRM College of Engineering, Kadapa, VNR Vignana Jyothi Institute of Engineering and Technology, Hyderabad, Guru Nanak Engineering College, Hyderabad and Nalla Narasimha Reddy Group of Institutions. He has also having experience as software engineer (SAP MM Consultant) for two years at SAT Infotech Pvt. Ltd. Hyderabad.

He has organized several Faculty Development Programs approved by ISTE/AICTE and also attended around 40 Faculty Development Programs in prestigious institutions like IITs, NITs, EDII and other Universities/Institutions. As convener/coordinator, he has organized many National level conferences and symposia during his career. Delivered many invited lectures in at institutions like JNTUH, Institution of Engineers, and other institutions.

Presently he is the convener for the Institution's Innovation Council, Industry Institution Interaction Cell, Incubation Center approved by MSME in the present institution (NNRG). Apart from the regular academics, he is regular practitioner of Yoga and certified trainer from Yoga Certification Board (YCB), Ministry of Ayush, New Delhi.

CHAPTER 1

Introduction to SIMULINK

1.0 WHAT IS SIMULINK?

Simulink is a graphical user interface platform that enables users to create mathematical models instantaneously. It provides simple means for solving complex mathematical equations without writing lengthy programmes.

The typical Simulink model is shown in Figure 1.1.

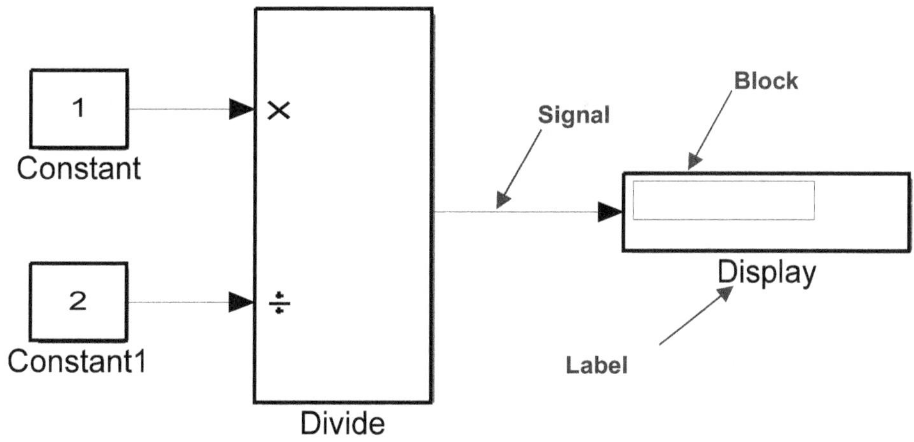

Figure 1.1 Typical Simulink model

Elements of Simulink model are given in Table 1.1.

Table 1.1 Elements of Simulink model

Blocks	Functions having input and output signals
Signals	Connects input/output between blocks
Labels	Applicable for blocks and signals They are not executable statements Useful for identification

1.1   MATLAB AND SIMULINK

Matlab and Simulink share a common platform, and hence problems can be solved in conjunction with both. Simulink needs to be initiated from MATLAB.

Example 1.1: Forced harmonic motion – Mass excitation

To obtain the response of a single degree of freedom (SDOF) system subjected to harmonic excitation with force magnitude of F_0 sin ωt shown in Figure 1.2.

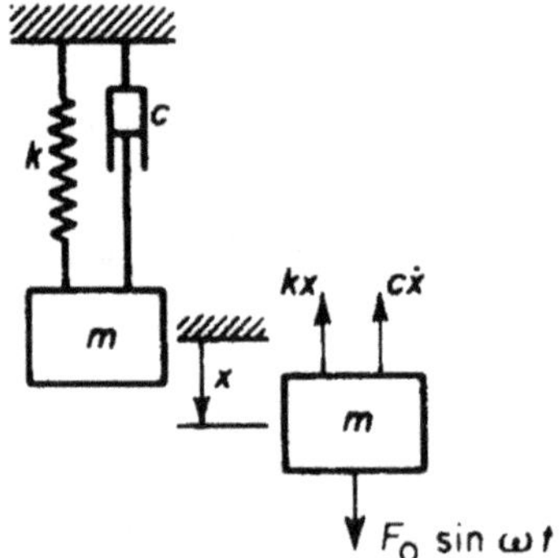

Figure 1.2 SDOF model of a system subjected to harmonic excitation

To consider the following parameters.

- m = 10 kg
- c = 200 Ns/m
- k = 100 N/m
- F_0 = 50 N
- r = 2
- Time duration = 20 seconds

Mathematical

From the free body diagram representation of the above mentioned system, the equation of motion can be expressed as

$$m\ddot{x} + c\dot{x} + kx = F_0 \operatorname{Sin}\omega t \qquad\qquad .....(1.1)$$

Where

> m: Mass
> $\ddot{x}$: Acceleration
> c: Damping coefficient
> $\dot{x}$: Velocity
> k: Stiffness
> x: Response of the system
> F_o: Amplitude
> ω: Excitation frequency
> t: Time

The following solution can be assumed.

$$x = X \sin (\omega t - \phi) \qquad\qquad .....(1.2)$$

Where

> X: Response amplitude
> ϕ: Phase difference between response and excitation force

The above two response parameters can be obtained by substituting equation 1.2 in equation 1.1 as given below.

$$X = \frac{F_0}{\sqrt{(k - m\omega^2)^2 + (c\omega)^2}} \qquad \qquad .....(1.3)$$

$$\varphi = \tan^{-1}\left(\frac{c\omega}{k - m\omega^2}\right) \qquad \qquad .....(1.4)$$

Taking the equation 1.3 and equation 1.4 in non-dimensional form, i.e. by dividing both numerator and denominator with k gives

$$X = \frac{\frac{F_0}{k}}{\sqrt{\left(1 - \frac{m\omega^2}{k}\right)^2 + \left(\frac{c\omega}{k}\right)^2}} \qquad \qquad .....(1.5)$$

$$\varphi = \tan^{-1}\left(\frac{\frac{c\omega}{k}}{1 - \frac{m\omega^2}{k}}\right) \qquad \qquad .....(1.6)$$

Further

$$Natural \text{ frequency, } \omega_n = \sqrt{\frac{k}{m}}$$

Critical damping coefficient, $c_c = 2m\omega_n$

$$Damping \text{ factor, } \zeta = \frac{c}{c_c}$$

$$\frac{c\,\omega}{k} = \frac{c}{c_c}\frac{c_c}{k}\omega = 2\,\zeta\,\frac{\omega}{\omega_n}$$

$$Frequency \text{ ratio, } r = \frac{\omega}{\omega_n}$$

Substituting the above relations in equations 1.5 and 1.6 gives

$$X = \frac{\frac{F_0}{k}}{\sqrt{(1 - r^2)^2 + (2\,\zeta\,r)^2}} \qquad \qquad .....(1.7)$$

$$\varphi = \tan^{-1}\left(\frac{2\,\zeta\,r}{1 - r^2}\right) \qquad \qquad .....(1.8)$$

Substituting equation 1.7 in equation 1.2 gives the expression for a response as follows

$$x = \frac{\frac{F_0}{k}}{\sqrt{(1 - r^2)^2 + (2\,\zeta\,r)^2}}\,\sin\,(\omega\,t - \varphi) \qquad \qquad .....(1.9)$$

Solution using MATLAB

Equations 1.8 and 1.9 are programmed in Matlab and the associated code is given below.

```
clf

clear
```

```
m=10;
c=200;
k=100;
F=50;
wn=(k/m)^0.5;
w=2*wn;
r=w/wn;
z=c/(2*m*wn);
r2=r^2;
pi=atan((2*z*r2)/(1-r2));
den=((1-r2)^2+(2*z*r)^2)^0.5;
t=0:0.1:20;
num=(F/k)*sin(w*t-pi);
x=num/den;
plot(t,x)
```

Executing the above Matlab code produces a result as shown in Figure 1.3.

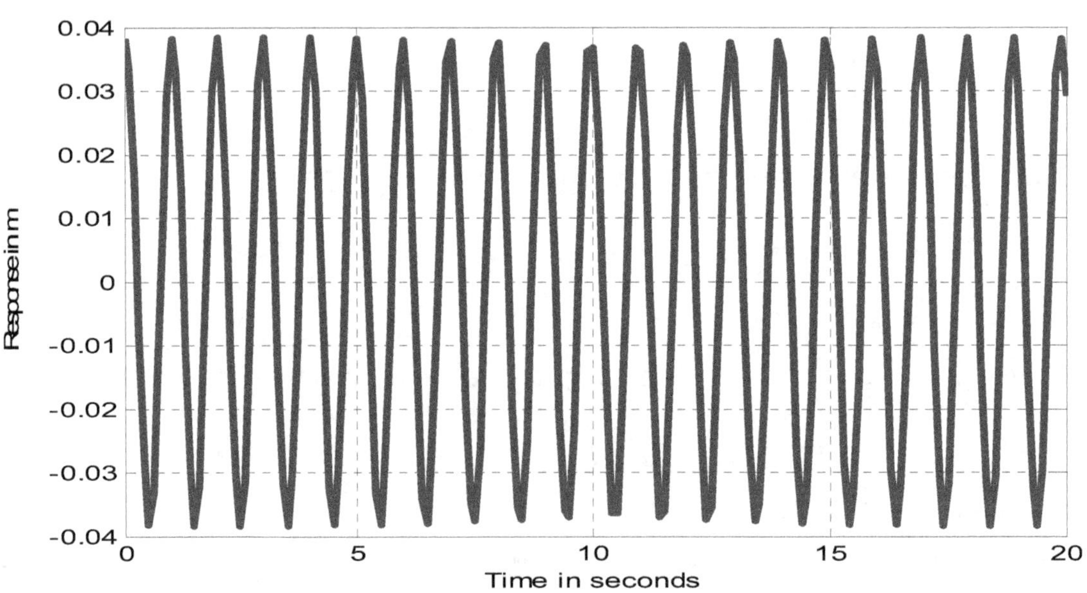

Figure 1.3 Response plot - Matlab

Solution using Simulink

Substituting the values in equation 1.1 gives.

$$10\,\ddot{x} + 200\,\dot{x} + 100\,x = 50\,Sin\,\omega\,t \qquad .....(1.10)$$

Rewriting same as

$$5\,Sin\,\omega\,t - 20\,\dot{x} - 10\,x = \ddot{x} \qquad .....(1.11)$$

The logic for solving equation 1.11 using Simulink is given in Table 1.2.

Table 1.2 Logic for solving equation 1.11 using Simulink

Component of equation	Operation needs to be performed	Feature needed in Simulink
Velocity, $\dot{x}$	Integration of acceleration, $\ddot{x}$	Integration
-20 $\dot{x}$	Multiplying (Gain) $\dot{x}$ with -20	Gain with a value of -20
Displacement response, x	Integration of velocity, $\dot{x}$	Integration
-10 x	Multiplying (Gain) x with -10	Gain with a value of -10
Sin (ωt)	Sinusoidal	Sine wave function
5 Sin (ωt)	Multiplying (Gain) sin (ωt) with 5	Gain with a value of 5
$5\,Sin\,\omega\,t + (-20\,\dot{x}) + (-10\,x)$	Summation	Sum
$5\,Sin\,\omega\,t + (-20\,\dot{x}) + (-10\,x) = \ddot{x}$	Equating evaluated LHS expression to acceleration, integrating which of same gives velocity and further integrating gives displacement response	

    Simulink needs to be initiated from Matlab. After entering into Matlab main window, i.e. command window, the following command needs to be typed as shown in Figure 1.4.

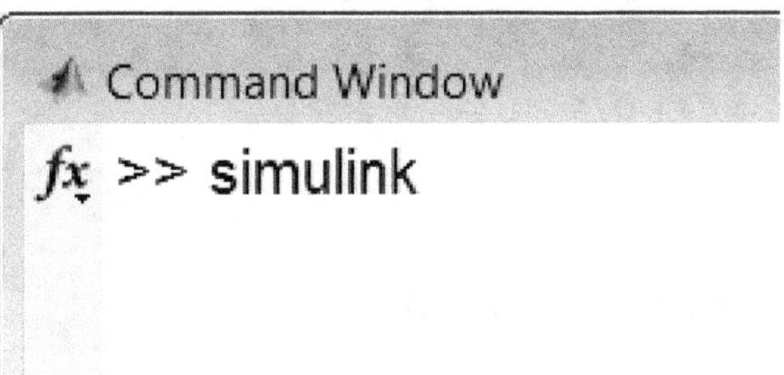

Figure 1.4 Initiating Simulink from Matlab.

Then Simulink library browser window will appear as shown in Figure 1.5.

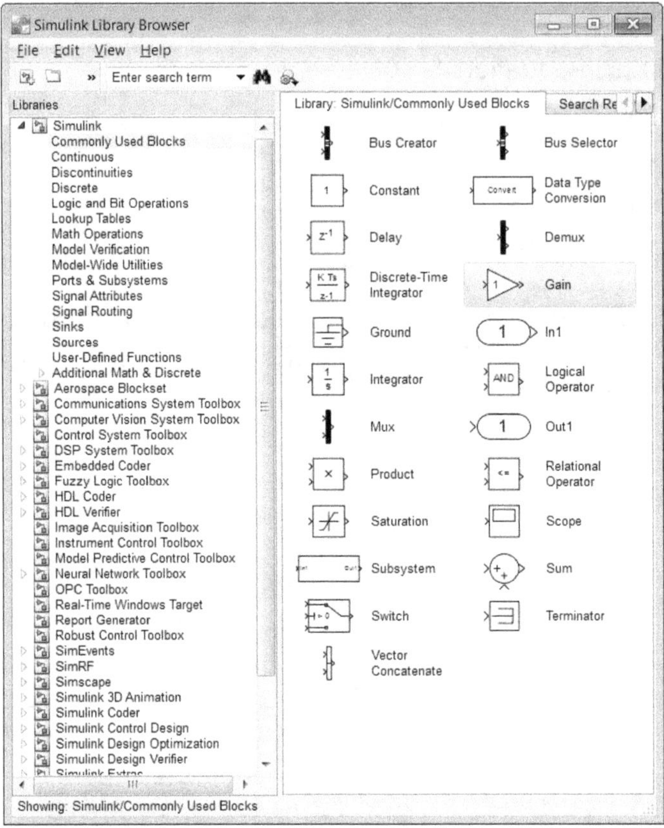

Figure 1.5 Simulink library browser window

Other way is to select Simulink library directly from Simulink on top in command window as shown in Figure 1.6.

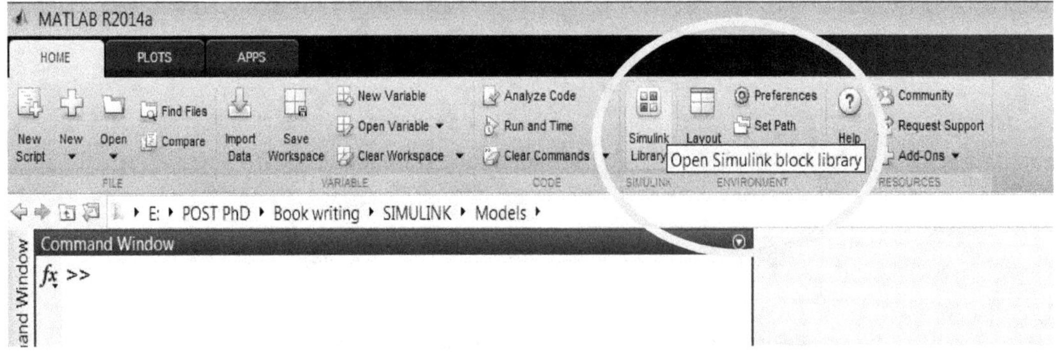

Figure 1.6 Selection of Simulink browser directly from the top menu in the command window

A New Simulink model file has to be created using the following steps.

File – New – Model

The same is shown in Figure 1.7.

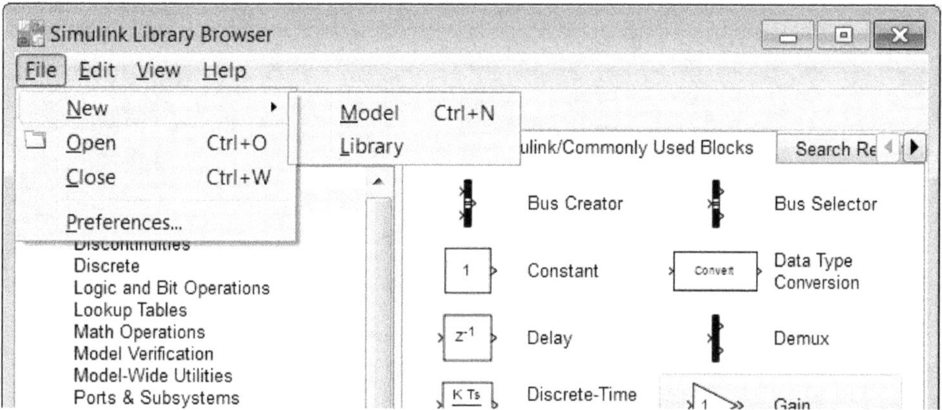

Figure 1.7 Creating new Simulink model

Then a window shown in Figure 1.8 will appear.

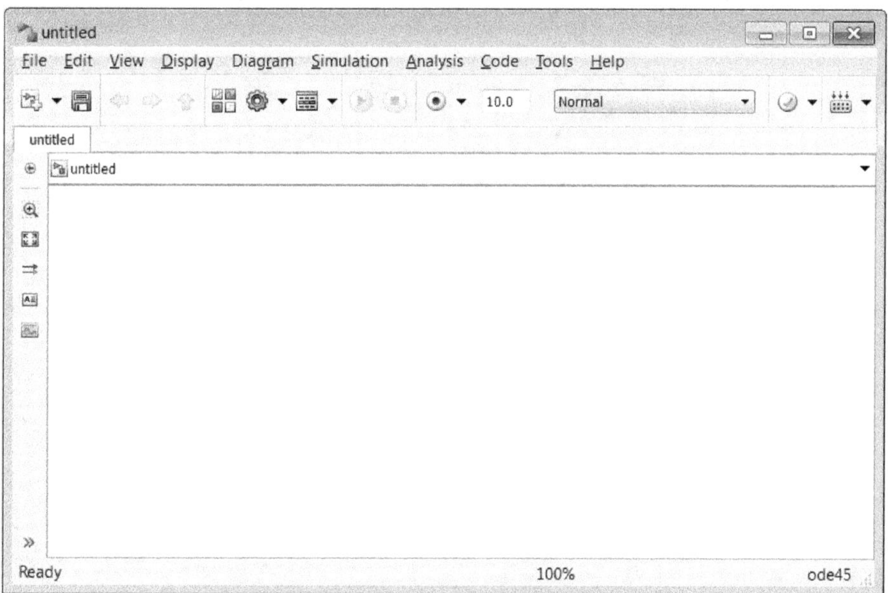

Figure 1.8 Creating new Simulink model

Select **commonly used blocks – sources – sine wave** block and drag the same using left mouse button and position it on untitled window as shown in Figure 1.9.

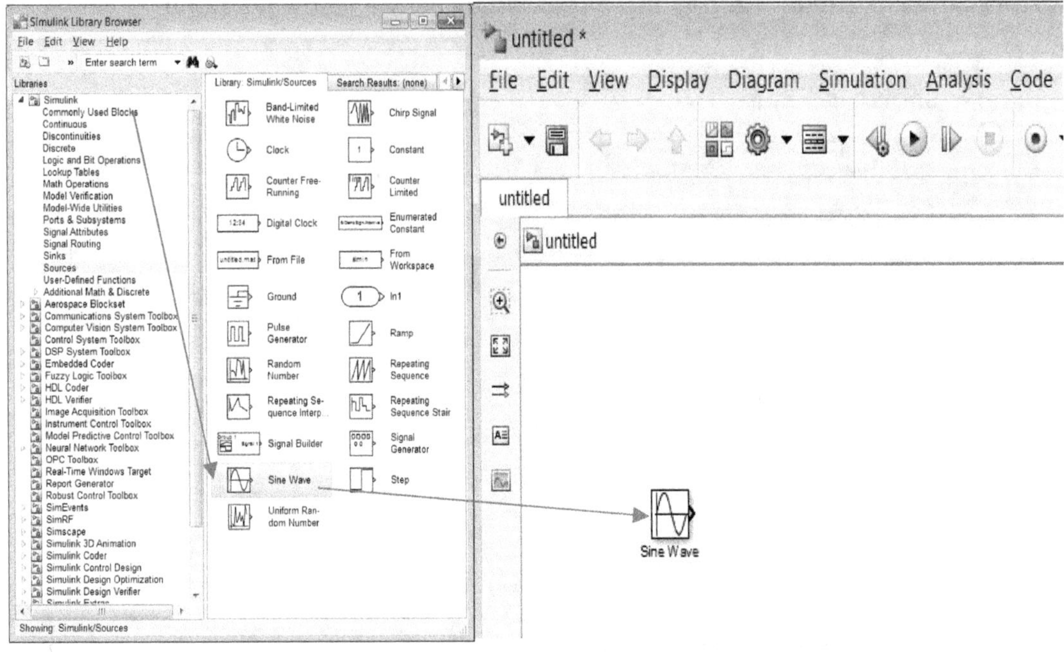

Figure 1.9 Sine wave block positioned in the model

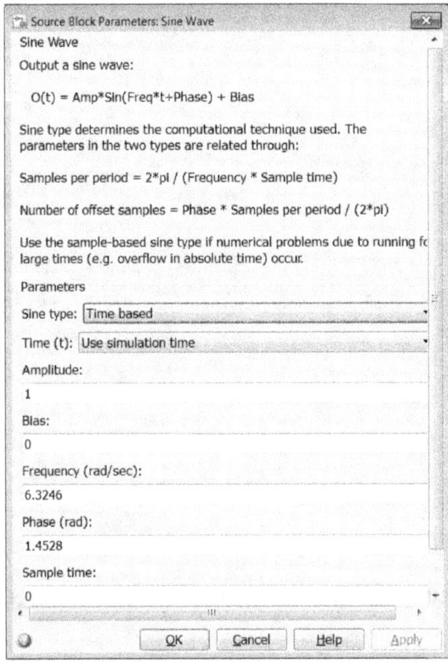

Figure 1.10 Function block parameters for sine wave block

From Matlab, the following parameters are computed, and the same is used for Simulink.

Excitation frequency, ω = 6.3246 rad/sec

Phase difference, ϕ = -1.4528 rad

Sine wave block needs to be double clicked to get associated properties window in which values **(Frequency = 6.3246 rad/sec and phase = 1.4528 rad/sec & rest are to be left with default values)** are to be entered as shown in Figure 1.10.

Note: A positive value is considered for phase as software assumes sin $(\omega t+\phi)$ whereas formulation is in the form of sin $(\omega t-\phi)$ with the actual value of ϕ is -1.4528.

Then three **gain** blocks from **commonly used blocks** are to be positioned as shown in Figure 1.11.

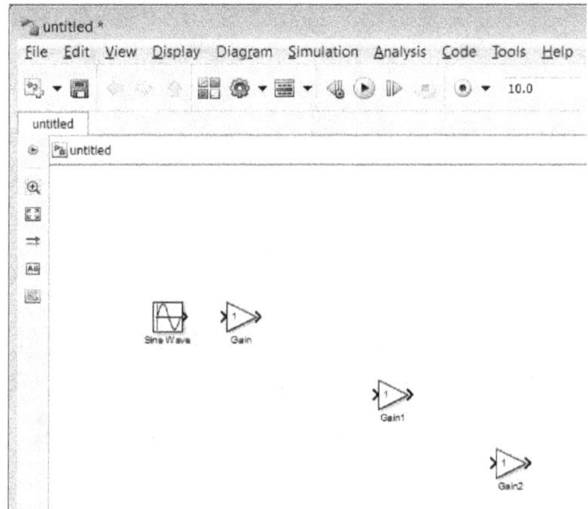

Figure 1.11 Gain blocks

Double click **gain** block (One RHS to **sine wave** block) and enter the value **(Gain = 5)** in the properties window as shown in Figure 1.12.

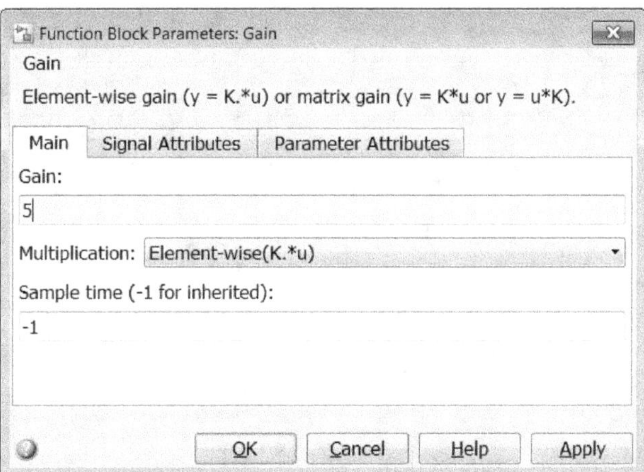

Figure 1.12 Function block parameters for gain block

Select **gain1** block (One middle bottom), then press a right mouse button and choose the options **rotate & flip - flip block** from popup menu with which orientation of **gain1** block will get changed as shown in Figure 1.13.

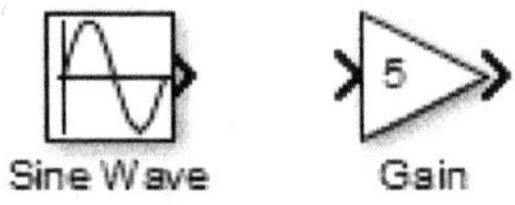

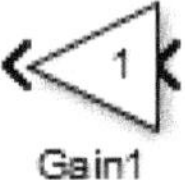

Figure 1.13 Orientation of gain1 block

Double click the **gain1** block and change its **gain** property to -20 from the resulting property window. Change the orientation of **gain2** block also the same as for **gain1** block. Change the **gain** property to -10 for **gain2** block by double clicking it.

Position **Add** block (**From math operations**) RHS to **gain** block as shown in Figure 1.14.

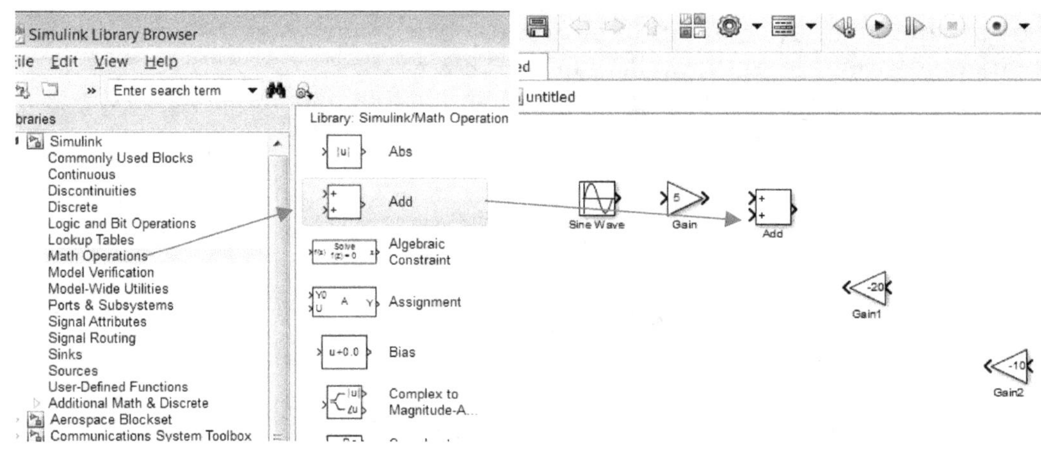

Figure 1.14 Add block

Double click **add** block and type **+++** under **list of signs** property (**+++** should appear) as shown in Figure 1.15.

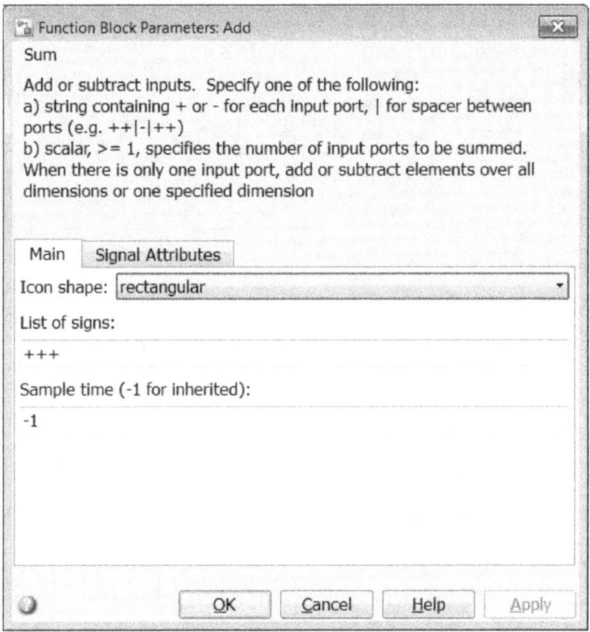

Figure 1.15 Function block parameters for add block

Position two **integrator** blocks (From commonly used blocks) RHS to gain block as shown in Figure 1.16.

Note:

- Copy-paste operations can be performed to create identical blocks from one block.

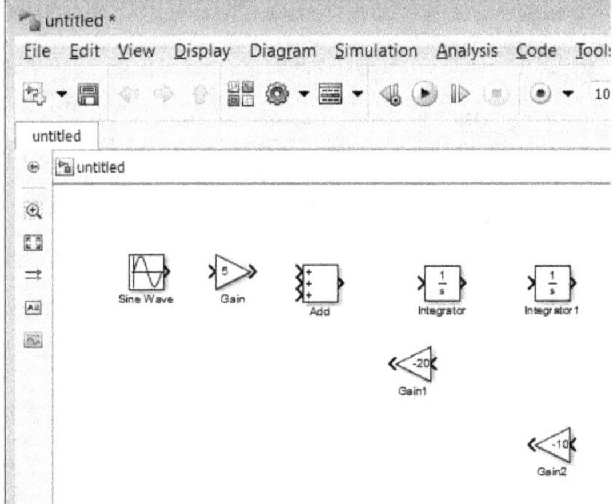

Figure 1.16 Integrator blocks

Position **scope** block (From **sinks**) RHS to **integrator1** block as shown in Figure 1.17.

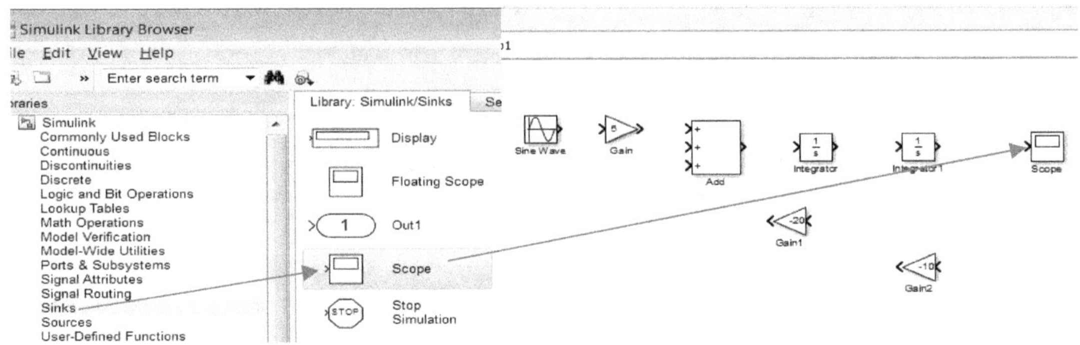

Figure 1.17 Scope block

Now all blocks need to be connected appropriately. For connecting two blocks
- The cursor needs to be positioned on the output arrow of the first block
- Press the left mouse button
- Drag the cursor on to input arrow of the second block
- Release the left mouse button

While leading cursor from input arrow of the first block to output arrow of the second block, connecting line becomes dotted red and gets converted into solid black line if a connection is established properly otherwise, it remains as a dotted red line.

Note:

- Care is to be exercised to ensure all solid black connecting lines between blocks before running the Simulink model file. While the left mouse button is pressed drag over all blocks to select them, press the right mouse button and select format and then font style so as to change the font of names of blocks as desired.

Simulink model file with all connections between blocks is shown in Figure 1.18.

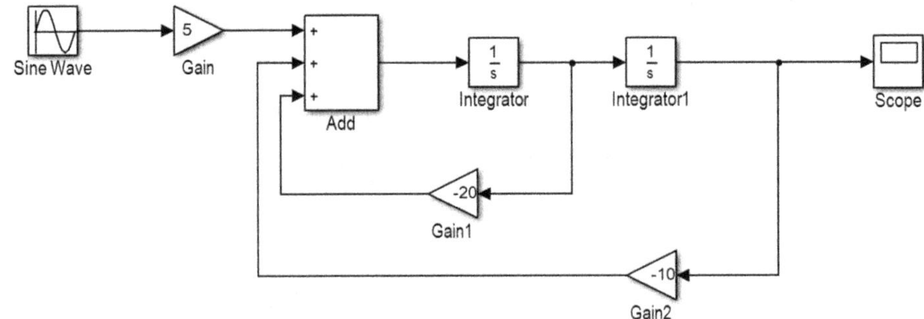

Figure 1.18 Simulink model file

Type 20 in **simulation stop time** window on top, save the model with a file name and run the model (Green arrow button) as shown in Figure 1.19.

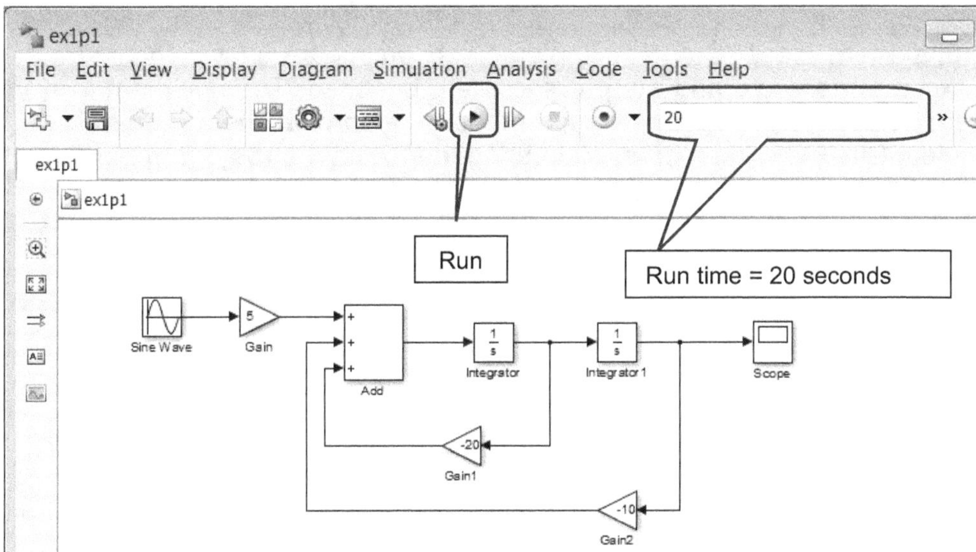

Figure 1.19 Run and Run time features

Once the run button is pressed, Simulink model file gets executed. Then double click **scope** block. A graph will be displayed which will not be fit on the screen, and hence select the auto scale icon on the top side of the graph. The final result thus produced is shown in Figure 1.20.

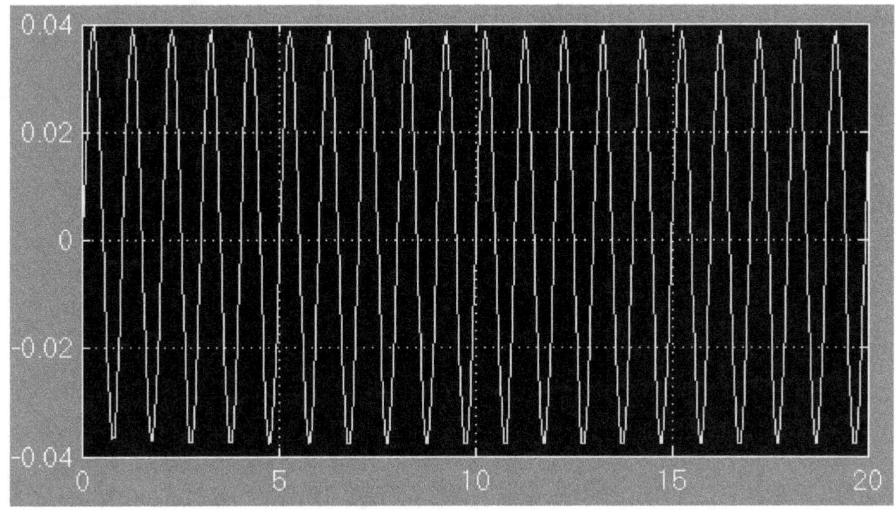

Figure 1.20 Response plot - Simulink

1.2 SIMPLIFYING COMPLEX SIMULINK MODELS

Often Simulink models will have more number of blocks with connections which may create an ambiguity. In such cases model can be simplified by bunching some blocks using **subsystem** block. Same is implemented on model shown in Figure 1.17. All blocks except **sine wave** and **scope** blocks are bunched. To implement this, the said blocks are selected by dragging the left mouse button over them. While those blocks are selected, Ctrl + G can be pressed to bring them within **subsystem** block, as shown in Figure 1.21.

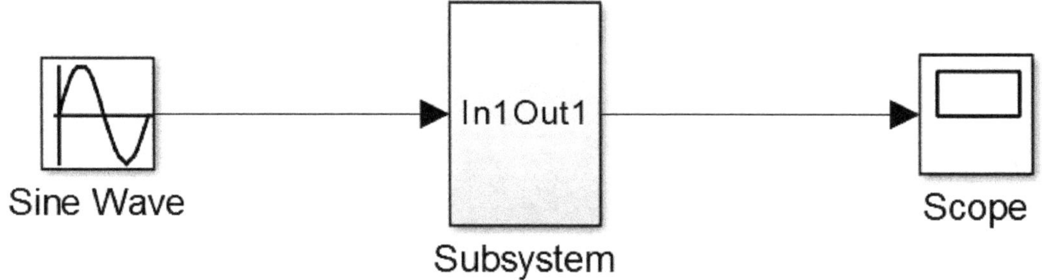

Figure 1.21 Simplified Simulink model using subsystem block

By double clicking **subsystem** block model changes with **sine wave** and **scope** blocks replaced by **In1** and **Out1**, respectively, as shown in Figure 1.22. **In1** and **Out1** represent input and output to **subsystem** block.

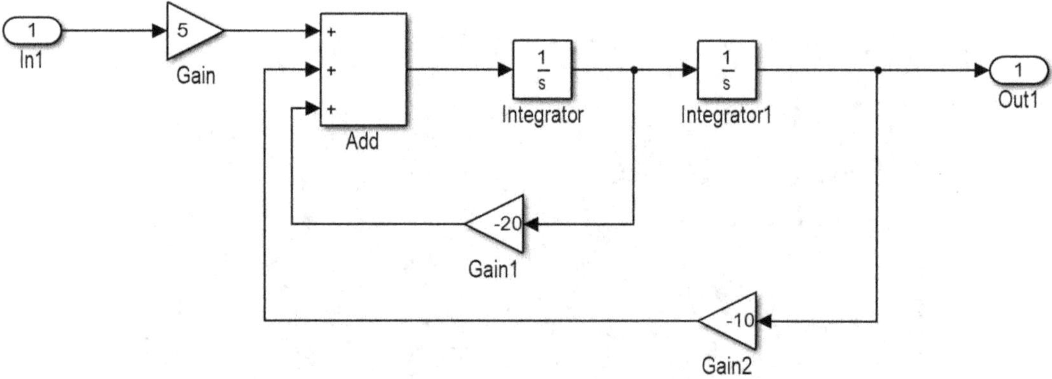

Figure 1.22 Expanded Simulink model - Subsystem block

In1, Out1 and **subsystem** blocks can be found from **commonly used blocks**.

1.3   MANAGEMENT OF VARIABLES IN SIMULINK

Values for variables lying in Simulink blocks can be assigned from Matlab. This feature enables smooth control over changing the values for variables, and this is illustrated below.

The typical Simulink model is shown in Figure 1.23.

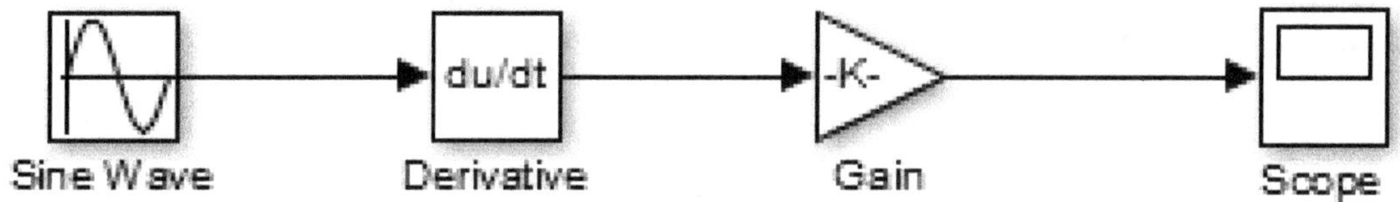

Figure 1.23 Typical Simulink model

The gain property consists of two variables 'a' and 'b'. Values for these variables have to be specified from Matlab before running Simulink model, and after that, they reside in the matlab workspace. Gain block parameters and Matlab work space are shown in Figure 1.24.

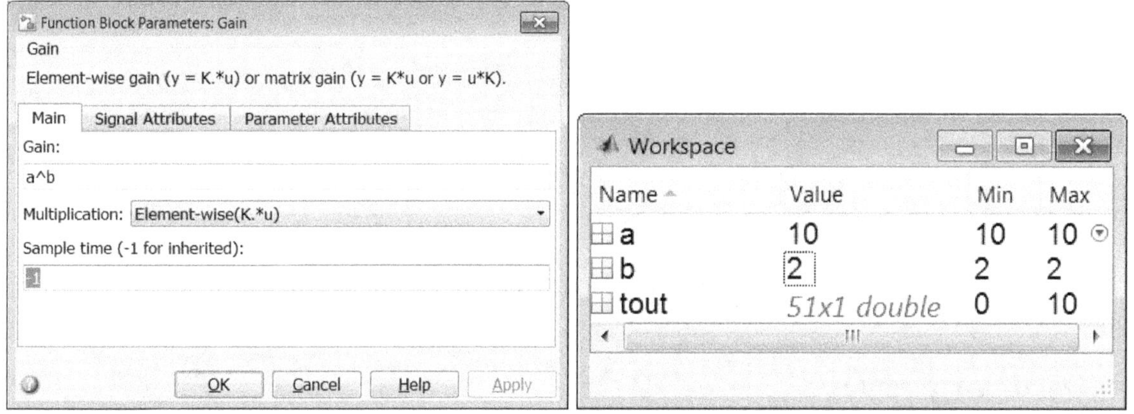

Figure 1.24 Function block parameters for gain block and matlab workspace

Values for variables can be changed comfortably from matlab workspace, and the Simulink model can be activated to study the influence of change in the values on results.

1.4   LABELLING VARIOUS ENTITIES

The simulink model, can be labelled for a description of the model. Double clicking the empty space anywhere in the model will enable a user to type the label. Alternatively, annotation icon on left side of model window also can be used to do so. Signals meant for connecting blocks also can be labelled, and signal line has to be double clicked for specifying the label. Labels can be edited by a pop up menu, which gets activated by the right mouse button. Simulink model shown in Figure 1.23 with labels to different entities is shown in Figure 1.25.

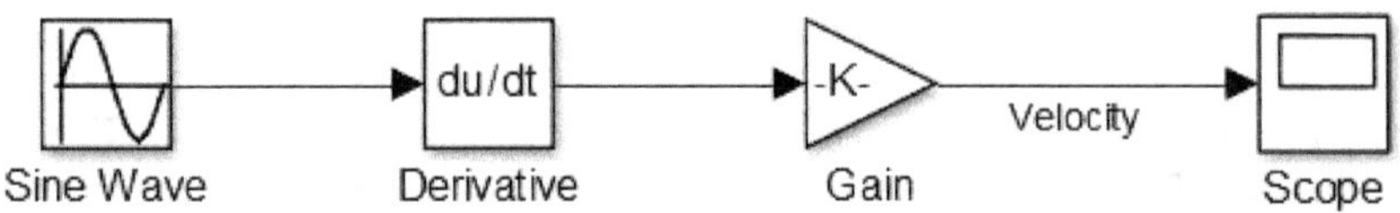

Figure 1.25 Simulink model with labels

1.5 FORMATTING BLOCKS

Blocks can be formatted by activating pop up menu. Font size, background colors and other parameters can be changed. Simulink model shown in Figure 1.23 after adding background colors to blocks is shown in Figure 1.26.

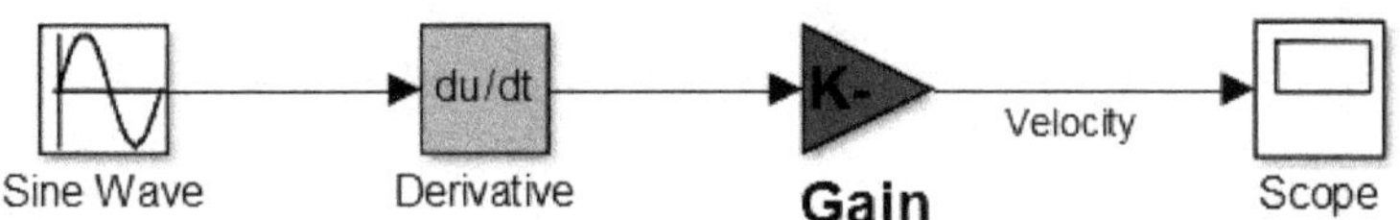

Figure 1.26 Simulink model with formatted blocks

1.6 QUICK OPTIONS

Options available in Simulink for performing quick operations on entities like blocks, signals, etc are given in Table 1.3.

Table 1.3 Options available in Simulink for performing quick operations

Sl. No.	Operation to be performed	Quick option
1.	For copying the entity	Select the entity and then drag the same with Ctrl + left mouse button
2.	For increasing/decreasing the size of block along diagonal while maintaining same width and height	Shift + Drag the block

Contd...

Sl. No.	Operation to be performed	Quick option
3.	For increasing/decreasing the size of block along width/ height	Ctrl + Drag the block
4.	To flip the block	Ctrl + Drag the block
5.	To rotate the block clockwise	Ctrl + R
6.	To rotate the block counterclockwise	Ctrl + Shift + R
7.	For connecting two blocks	Select first block, then Ctrl + select second block
8.	To create subsystem for bunch of blocks	Select the blocks Ctrl + G
9.	To move any label	To drag with left mouse button
10.	To change font of name for block	To drag with left mouse button over all blocks, right mouse button, format, font style
11.	To run simulation	Ctrl + T
12.	To stop simulation	Ctrl + Shift + T
13.	To zoom in	Ctrl + +
14.	To zoom out	Ctrl + -
15.	To zoom to 100%	Alt + 1
16.	Fit view	Press space bar
17.	To move model within screen	Space bar + drag with left mouse button

1.7 SUMMARY

This chapter brings out an overview of Simulink. Basic differences between matlab and Simulink are illustrated with the aid of an example. Methodology for simplifying complex Simulink models is elaborated. Various means for labelling different entities in a Simulink model are discussed. Procedure for formatting blocks is outlined. Further various options available for quick access of Simulink models are highlighted.

CHAPTER 2

Basic Mathematical Operations

2.0 MATHEMATICAL OPERATIONS

Mathematical operations play a vital role in modeling and solving complex mathematical equations in any form whether it is a simple algebraic equation or it could be a higher order differential equation. These operations are also needed for statistical data estimation. This chapter brings out performing various mathematical operations using Simulink.

2.1 ADDITION

To begin with simplest one among mathematical operations i.e. addition is considered. An illustrative example is given below.

EXAMPLE 2.1

To build a Simulink model for addition of sin θ and cos θ where θ = 90⁰.

Simulink model is shown in Figure 2.1.

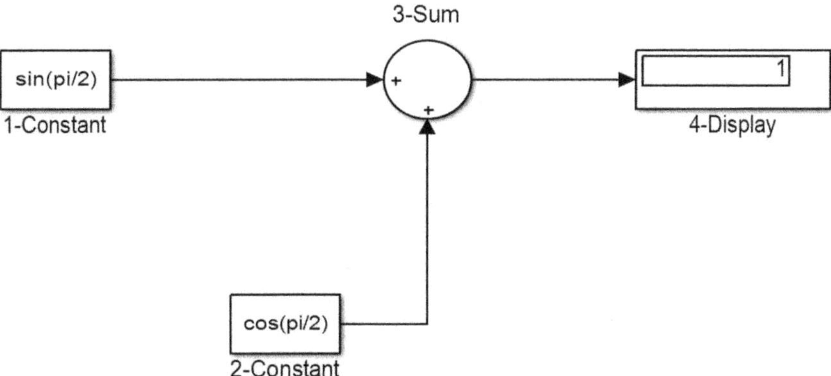

Figure 2.1 Simulink model for addition

Constant block is used for defining sin(pi/2) and cos(pi/2) as it evaluates such functions. **Sum** block is used for addition. Further **display** block is used for displaying the result.

Details of blocks are given in Table 2.1.

Table 2.1 Details of blocks - Addition

Name of block in model	Name of block in Simulink library	Source	Properties
1-Constant	Constant	Commonly used blocks	Constant value = sin(pi/2)
2-Constant	Constant	Commonly used blocks	Constant value = cos(pi/2)
3-Sum	Sum	Commonly used blocks	----
4-Display	Display	Sinks	----

After building the model it needs to be activated through **Run** button. Then the result will be displayed in **display** block as shown in Figure 2.1.

Note:

- Properties as stated in the above table can be obtained by double clicking particular block. Upon doing so function block parameters window will appear where the specified properties can be defined. It is to be noted that same is applicable for all chapters.
- Shape of **Sum** block can be either round or rectangular which can be chozen from icon shape option in function block parameters. Same block can be used for subtraction also by specifying '–' sign in list of signs option. 'l' sign can be specified in list of signs for creating space between input signals in the block. For example specifying +++l--l+++ and icon shape as rectangular will display the **sum** block as shown below.

For any reason if some blocks are deleted and attempt is made to run the model, it will yield to warning message. In such cases it can be managed with **ground** block. Model after removal of **1-constant** block and same after addition of **ground** block is shown in Figure 2.2.

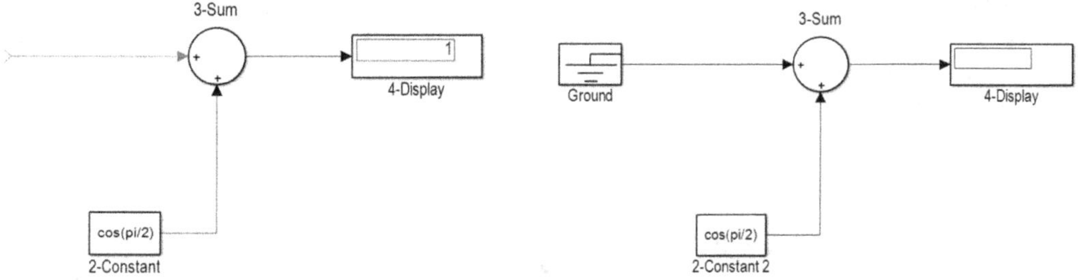

Figure 2.2 Simulink models with out 1-constant block and with ground block

Ground block can be sourced from **commonly used blocks** and it doesn't need any properties to be assigned.

In case if any block is removed in output side, it can be managed with **terminator** block. Same implemented for previous model is shown in Figure 2.3.

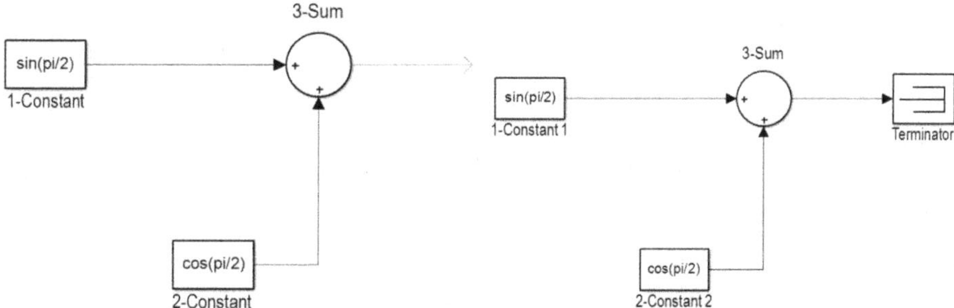

Figure 2.3 Simulink models without and with terminator block

Terminator block can be sourced from **commonly used blocks** and it doesn't need any properties to be assigned.

2.2 PRODUCT

Multiplication is another mathematical function and example for same with respect to trigonometric quantities in Simulink is given below.

EXAMPLE 2.2

To build a Simulink model for multiplication of cos θ and tan θ where $\theta = 180^0$.

Simulink model is shown in Figure 2.4.

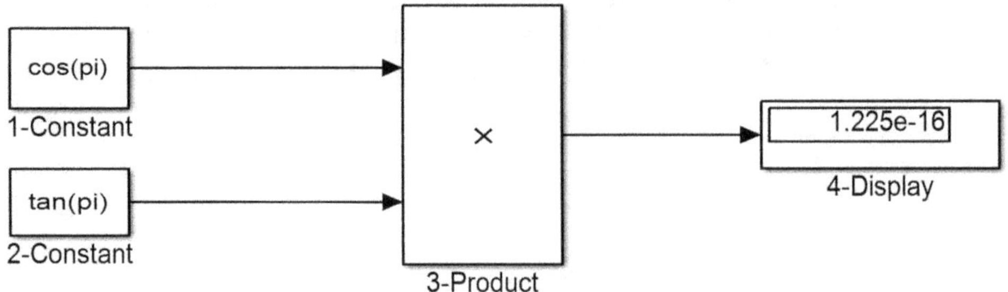

Figure 2.4 Simulink model for multiplication

Details of blocks are given in Table 2.2.

Table 2.2 Details of blocks - Multiplication

Name of block in model	Name of block in Simulink library	Source	Properties
1-Constant	Constant	Commonly used blocks	Constant value = cos(pi)
2-Constant	Constant	Commonly used blocks	Constant value = tan(pi)
3-Product	Product	Commonly used blocks	----
4-Display	Display	Sinks	----

2.3 DIVISION

Division of two trigonometric expressions whose values are defined through **constant** block is explained below.

EXAMPLE 2.3

To build a Simulink model for division of sin θ and tan θ where $\theta = 180^0$.

Simulink model is shown in Figure 2.5.

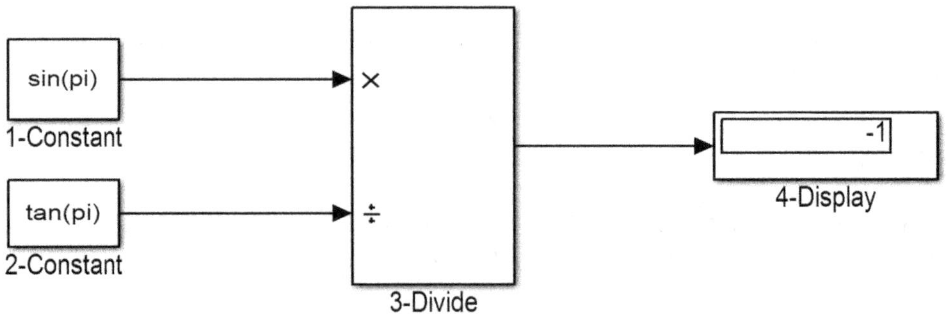

Figure 2.5 Simulink model for division

Details of blocks are given in Table 2.3.

Table 2.3 Details of blocks - Division

Name of block in model	Name of block in Simulink library	Source	Properties
1-Constant	Constant	Commonly used blocks	Constant value = sin(pi)
2-Constant	Constant	Commonly used blocks	Constant value = tan(pi)
3-Divide	Divide	Math operations	----
4-Display	Display	Sinks	----

2.4 SQUARE ROOT

Finding square root of numbers is one of the basic mathematical operations. An associated example is given below.

EXAMPLE 2.4

To build Simulink model for computing square root of 1, 2, 3, 4 and 9 and display the results which are above 1.5 and display 1.5 for those values which are less than or equal to 1.5.

For computing square root (**sqrt**) block is used. **Switch** block is needed for displaying the results as stated in the problem definition.

Simulink model is shown in Figure 2.6.

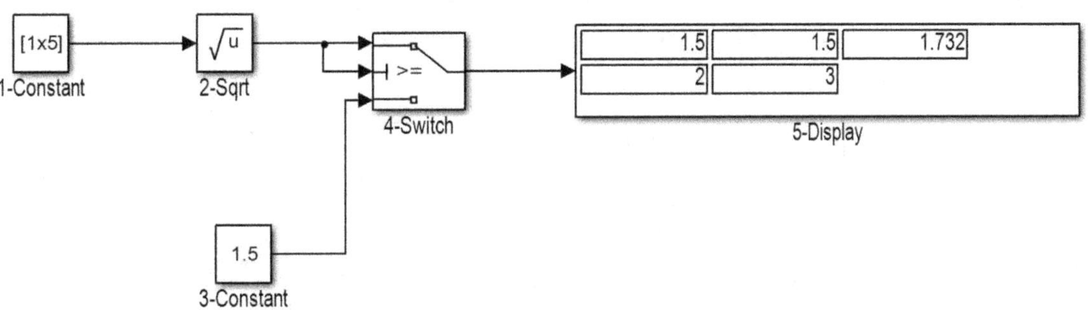

Figure 2.6 Simulink model – Square root

Details of blocks are given in Table 2.4.

Table 2.4 Details of blocks – Square root

Name of block in model	Name of block in Simulink library	Source	Properties
1-Constant	Constant	Commonly used blocks	Constant value = [1 2 3 4 9]
2-Sqrt	Sqrt	Math operations	Function: sqrt

Table 2.4 Contd...

Name of block in model	Name of block in Simulink library	Source	Properties
3-Constant	Constant	Commonly used blocks	Constant value = 1.5
4-Switch	Switch	Commonly used blocks	Criteria for passing first input: u2 >= Threshold Threshold: 1.5
5-Display	Display	Commonly used blocks	----

Logic

Switch block will have 3 input signals. First one and third one will be meant for feeding input whereas second one i.e. middle one is meant for defining logic. The moment square root is computed the result is fed to second signal so as to check with the criteria specified i.e. > = threshold (1.5). If the resulting value is $\geq$ 1.5 then same will be displayed in main display i.e. **5-display**. If the resulting value is not satisfying the criteria i.e. < 1.5, then the result will not be sent to **5-display** rather it will be ignored and input from third signal (3-constant) i.e. 1.5 will be sent to **5-display**.

2.5 COMPUTING FACTORIAL

Factorial for a given number can be computed in Simulink as given in the following example.

EXAMPLE 2.5

To build Simulink model for computing factorial of 9:

This can be achieved by **Product of elements** block. Associated Simulink model is shown in Figure 2.7.

Figure 2.7 Simulink model for computing factorial

Details of blocks are given in Table 2.5.

Table 2.5 Details of blocks – Factorial

Name of block in model	Name of block in Simulink library	Source	Properties
1-Constant	Constant	Commonly used blocks	[1 2 3 4 5 6 7 8 9]
2-Product of elements	Product of elements	Math operations	---
3-Display	Display	Sinks	---

2.6 TRIGONOMETRIC OPERATORS

Method of evaluating basic trigonometric functions is elaborated through the example below.

EXAMPLE 2.6

To build Simulink model which gives the following:

Sin (θ), sin^{-1} (Sin (θ)), cos(θ), cos^{-1} (cos (θ)), tan(θ), tan^{-1} (tan (θ)) for $\theta = 30^0$.

These are evaluated using **sin, asin, cos, acos, tan** and **atan** functions in **trigonometric function** block respectively. In addition to this **sincos** function is also used for evaluating both sin and cos together with single function.

Simulink model is shown in Figure 2.8.

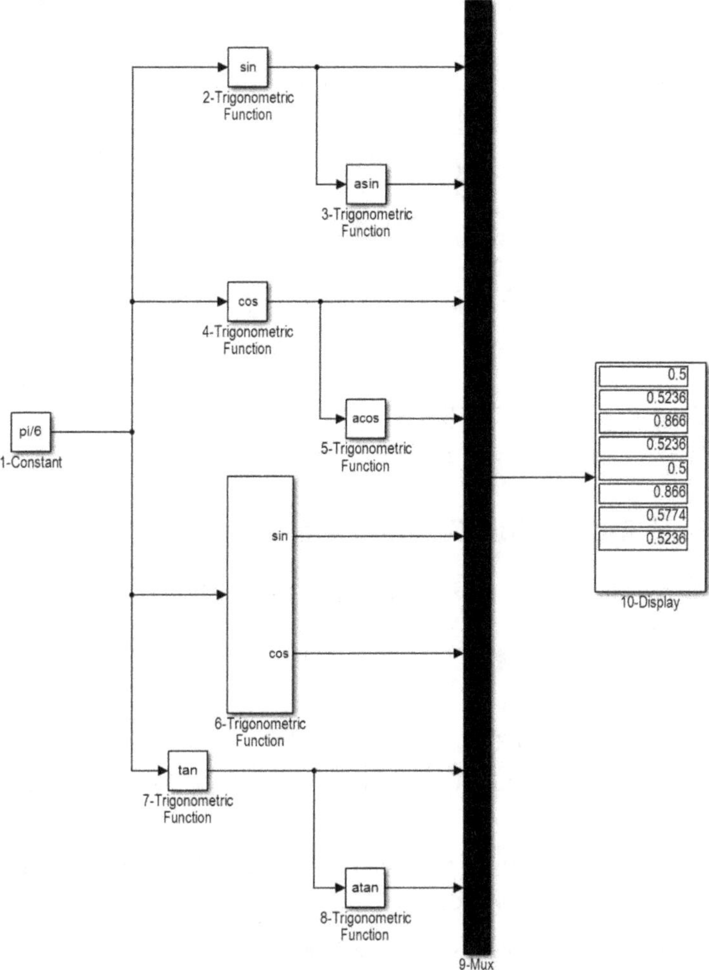

Figure 2.8 Simulink model – Trigonometric operators

Details of blocks are given in Table 2.6.

Table 2.6 Details of blocks - Trigonometric operators

Name of block in model	Name of block in Simulink library	Source	Properties
1-Constant	Constant	Commonly used blocks	Constant value = pi/6
2-Trigonometric function	Trigonometric function	Math operations	Function: sin
3-Trigonometric function	Trigonometric function	Math operations	Function: asin
4-Trigonometric function	Trigonometric function	Math operations	Function: cos
5-Trigonometric function	Trigonometric function	Math operations	Function: acos
6-Trigonometric function	Trigonometric function	Math operations	Function: sincos
7-Trigonometric function	Trigonometric function	Math operations	Function: tan
8-Trigonometric function	Trigonometric function	Math operations	Function: atan
9-Mux	Mux	Commonly used blocks	Number of inputs=8 Right mouse button – format - Show block name
10-Display	Display	Sinks	----

2.7 HYPERBOLIC TRIGONOMETRIC FUNCTIONS

Various functions are available in Simulink for evaluating hyperbolic expressions as given in the example below.

EXAMPLE 2.7

To build Simulink model which gives the following:

Sinh (θ), sinh^{-1} (Sinh (θ)), cosh (θ), cosh^{-1} (cosh (θ)), tanh (θ), tanh^{-1} (tanh (θ)) for $\theta = 5$.

These are evaluated using **sinh, asinh, cosh, acosh, tanh** and **atanh** functions in **trigonometric function** block respectively.

Associated Simulink model is shown in Figure 2.9.

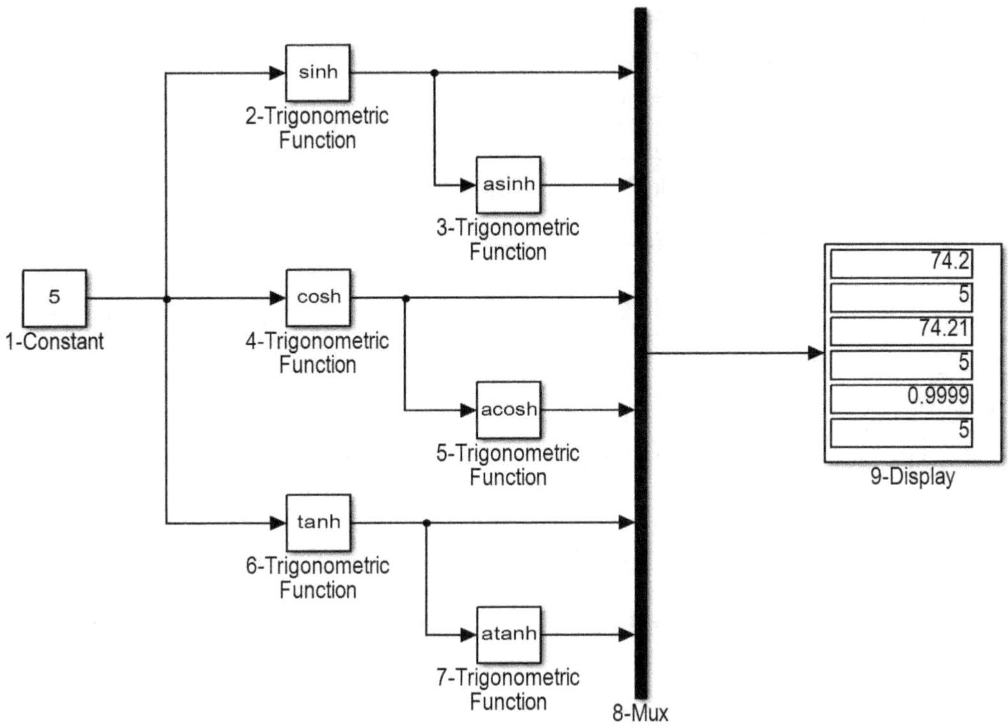

Figure 2.9 Simulink model for hyperbolic trigonometric functions

Details of blocks are given in Table 2.7.

Table 2.7 Details of blocks - Hyperbolic trigonometric functions

Name of block in model	Name of block in Simulink library	Source	Properties
1-Constant	Constant	Commonly used blocks	Constant value: 5
2-Trigonometric function	Trigonometric function	Math operations	Function: sinh
3-Trigonometric function	Trigonometric function	Math operations	Function: asinh
4-Trigonometric function	Trigonometric function	Math operations	Function: cosh
5-Trigonometric function	Trigonometric function	Math operations	Function: acosh

Table 2.7 Contd...

Name of block in model	Name of block in Simulink library	Source	Properties
6-Trigonometric function	Trigonometric function	Math operations	Function: tanh
7-Trigonometric function	Trigonometric function	Math operations	Function: atanh
8-Mux	Mux	Commonly used blocks	Number of inputs=6 Right mouse button – format - Show block name
9-Display	Display	Sinks	---

Note: Display blocks needs to be dragged to sufficient extent for displaying the results.

2.8 MATHEMATICAL FUNCTIONS

Simulink provides numerous mathematical functions and few of them are presented through the following example.

EXAMPLE 2.8

To build Simulink model for (i) Raising 10 to the power of x, (ii) x to the power of a, (iii) square root of sum of squares of x & b, (iv) Find the remainder after dividing x with c ignoring algebraic sign and (v) Find the remainder after dividing x with c considering algebraic sign.

Where
$$x = \begin{bmatrix} 4 & 6 & 8 & 10 \end{bmatrix}; \ a = 3; b = [1\,2\,3\,4]; c = [1\,2\,-3\,4]$$

(i) is addressed using **10^u** option in **math function** block, (ii) is addressed using **u^v** option in **math function** block (iii) is addressed using **hypot** option in **math function** block. (iv) To find the remainder after dividing x with c ignoring algebraic sign **rem** option in **math function** block is used and (v) For finding the remainder after dividing x with c considering algebraic sign **mod** option in **math function** block is used.

Mod block works as follows:

Mod(x,y) is x - n.*y where n = floor(x./y)

Associated Simulink model is shown in Figure 2.10.

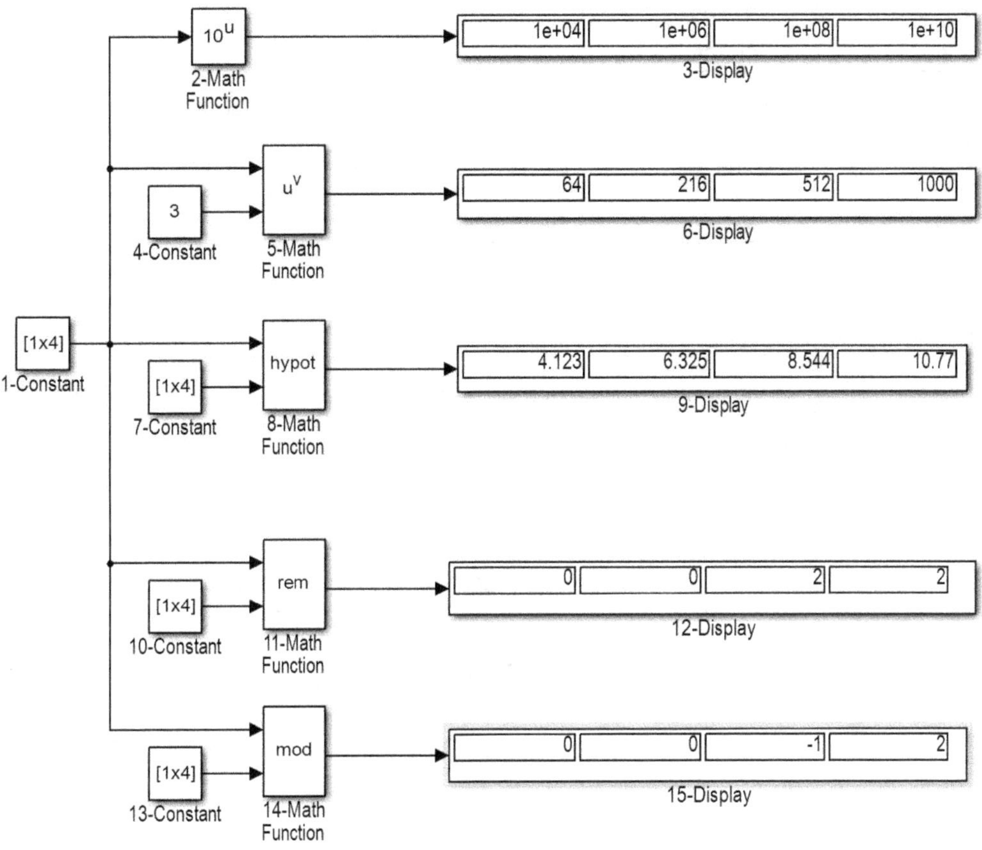

Figure 2.10 Simulink model for performing mathematical functions

Details of blocks are given in Table 2.8.

Table 2.8 Details of blocks - Mathematical functions

Name of block in model	Name of block in Simulink library	Source	Properties
1-Constant	Constant	Commonly used blocks	Constant value: [4 6 8 10]
2-Math function	Math function	Math operations	Function: 10^u
3-Display	Display	Sinks	---
4-Constant	Constant	Commonly used blocks	Constant value: 3
5-Math function	Math function	Math operations	Function: pow
6-Display	Display	Sinks	---
7-Constant	Constant	Commonly used blocks	Constant value: [1 2 3 4]

Table 2.8 *Contd...*

Name of block in model	Name of block in Simulink library	Source	Properties
8-Math function	Math function	Math operations	Function: hypot
9-Display	Display	Sinks	---
10-Constant	Constant	Commonly used blocks	Constant value: [1 2 -3 4]
11-Math function	Math function	Math operations	Function: rem
12-Display	Display	Sinks	---
13-Constant	Constant	Commonly used blocks	Constant value: [1 2 -3 4]
14-Math function	Math function	Math operations	Function: mod
15-Display	Display	Sinks	---

Note: **Display** blocks needs to be dragged to sufficient extent for displaying the results.

2.9   LOGARITHMIC AND EXPONENTIAL FUNCTIONS

Simulink also provides means for evaluating logarithmic and exponential functions and the same is illustrated in the following example.

EXAMPLE 2.9

To build Simulink model for evaluating the following and display '1' if the result is positive or display '0' if result is zero or display '-1' if result is negative.

(i) $\text{Log}_e(A(2))+e^{A(4)}$ (ii) $\text{Log}_e(A(1))+ \text{Log}_e(A(1))$ (iii) $\text{Log}_e(A(1))-e^{A(3)}$

Where

$$A = [1\ 4\ 1\ 9]$$

This can be achieved by **Sign** block. Associated Simulink model is shown in Figure.

Result displayed in **8-Display** block is '1' as the associated result is positive, whereas result displayed in **9-Display** block is '0' as the associated result is zero and result displayed in **10-Display** block is '-1' as the associated result is negative.

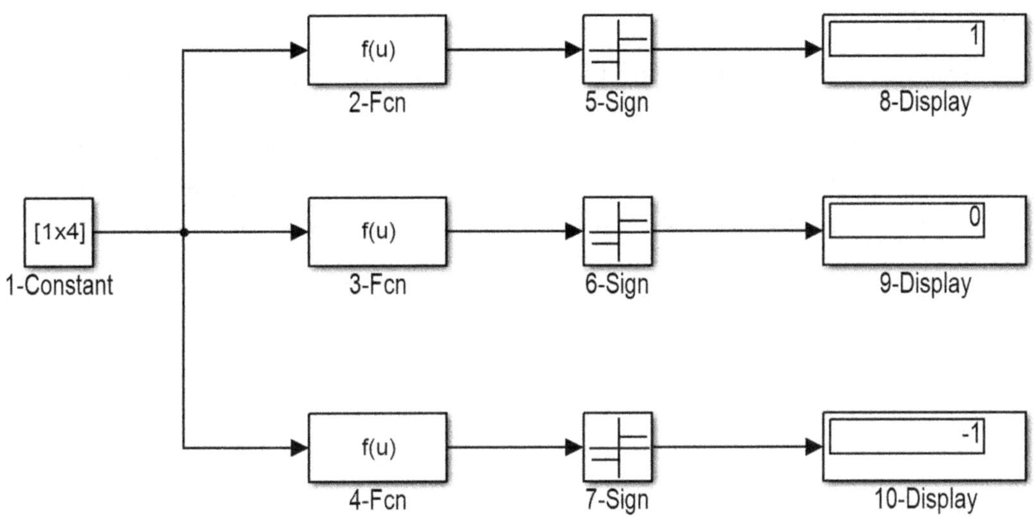

Figure 2.11 Simulink model for evaluating logarithmic and exponential functions

Details of blocks are given in Table.

Table 2.9 Details of blocks - Logarithmic and exponential functions

Name of block in model	Name of block in Simulink library	Source	Properties
1-Constant	Constant	Commonly used blocks	[1 4 1 9]
2-Fcn	Fcn	User defined functions	log(u(2))+exp(u(4))
3-Fcn	Fcn	User defined functions	log(u(1))+log(u(1))
4-Fcn	Fcn	User defined functions	log(u(1))-exp(u(3))
5-Sign	Sign	Math operations	---
6-Sign	Sign	Math operations	---
7-Sign	Sign	Math operations	---
8-Display	Display	Sinks	---
9-Display	Display	Sinks	---
10-Display	Display	Sinks	---

2.10 SUMMARY

Illustrative examples are provided for performing basic mathematical operations like addition, multiplication, division, square root, factorial in Simulink. Implementation of trigonometric operators and hyperbolic trigonometric functions is also mentioned. Building Simulink models with various mathematical functions is also elaborated. Also the illustrative example for evaluating logarithmic and exponential functions is included.

CHAPTER 3

Matrices

3.0 MATRICES

Applications of matrices are numerous in any field namely engineering, science, finance, statistics and also in many parts of mathematics. Matrices play key role in analyzing systems which are characterized with the aid of linear equations. Moreover it is comfortable in transforming algebraic equations to matrices and then solving the same. Matrices are also useful for graphical representation of behavior of certain systems. This chapter brings out performing various matrix operations with the aid of Simulink.

3.1 MATRIX MULTIPLICATION

Matrix multiplication is significant in general matrix operations. It is used in studying the behavior of linear systems. Further it is extremely useful for transformation of system of coordinates.

EXAMPLE 3.1

To build Simulink models for multiplying two matrices, matrix with vector and matrix with a scalar as given below:

$$(i)\begin{bmatrix}2&7&6\\4&9&3\\1&5&2\end{bmatrix} \times \begin{bmatrix}3&2&5\\7&1&6\\8&4&3\end{bmatrix} \quad (ii)\begin{bmatrix}2&7&6\\4&9&3\\1&5&2\end{bmatrix} \times \begin{bmatrix}3\\7\\8\end{bmatrix} \quad (iii)\begin{bmatrix}3&2&5\\7&1&6\\8&4&3\end{bmatrix} \times 2$$

Simulink model for case (i) is shown in Figure 3.1.

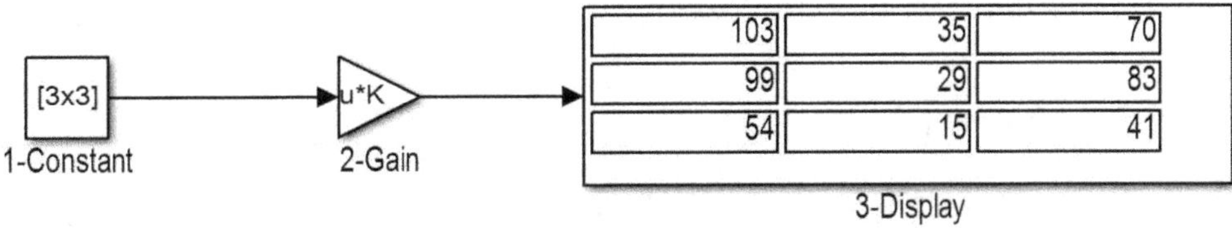

Figure 3.1 Simulink for matrix multiplication – Case (i)

Details of blocks are given in Table 3.1.

Table 3.1 Details of blocks for matrix multiplication – Case (i)

Name of block in model	Name of block in Simulink library	Source	Properties
1-Constant	Constant	Commonly used blocks	Constant value: [2 7 6; 4 9 3; 1 5 2]
2-Gain	Gain	Commonly used blocks	Gain: [3 2 5; 7 1 6; 8 4 3] Multiplication: Matrix(u*K)
3-Display	Display	Sinks	----

Simulink model for case (ii) is shown in Figure 3.2.

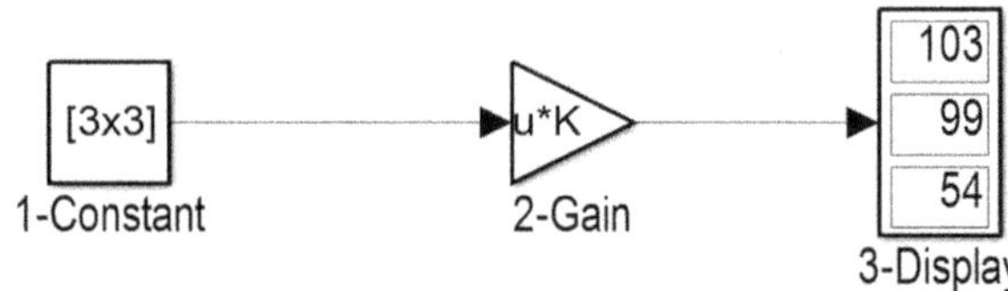

Figure 3.2 Simulink for matrix multiplication – Case (ii)

Details of blocks are given in Table 3.2.

Table 3.2 Details of blocks for matrix multiplication – Case (ii)

Name of block in model	Name of block in Simulink library	Source	Properties
1-Constant	Constant	Commonly used blocks	Constant value: [2 7 6; 4 9 3; 1 5 2]
2-Gain	Gain	Commonly used blocks	Gain: [3 7 8]' Multiplication: Matrix(u*K)
3-Display	Display	Sinks	----

Simulink model for case (iii) is shown in Figure 3.3.

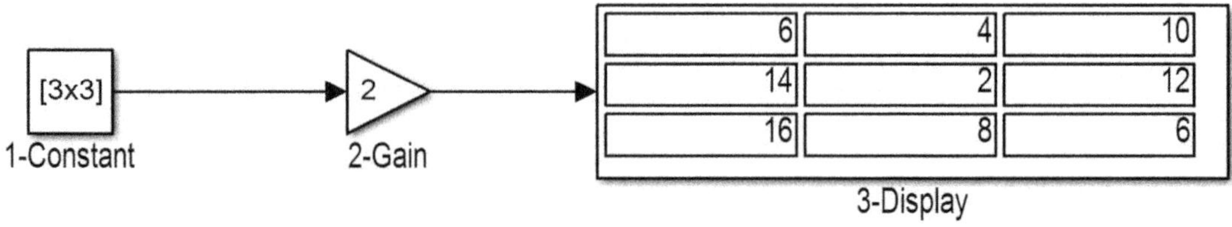

Figure 3.3 Simulink for matrix multiplication – Case (iii)

Details of blocks are given in Table 3.3.

Table 3.3 Details of blocks for matrix multiplication – Case (iii)

Name of block in model	Name of block in Simulink library	Source	Properties
1-Constant	Constant	Commonly used blocks	Constant value: [2 7 6; 4 9 3; 1 5 2]
2-Gain	Gain	Commonly used blocks	Gain: 2 Multiplication: Element-wise(K.*u)
3-Display	Display	Sinks	----

Note: For **gain** block Multiplication option has to be set to Matrix(K*u) if matrix multiplication is needed in reverse direction i.e. if the requirement is to multiply matrix specified in **gain** block with matrix specified in **constant** block.

3.2 DOT PRODUCT

Dot product is nothing but the addition of products of the corresponding elements of the two vectors.

EXAMPLE 3.2

To build Simulink model for performing dot product of A & B and C & D independently and then evaluating the ratio of dot product of A & B and dot product of C & D:

Where

$$A = [3\ 7\ 1\ 9];\ \ B = [5\ 2\ 8\ 4];\ \ C = [1\ 3\ 1\ 2];\ \ D = [2\ 1\ 3\ 4]$$

This can be achieved by **Dot product** block. Associated Simulink model is shown in Figure 3.4.

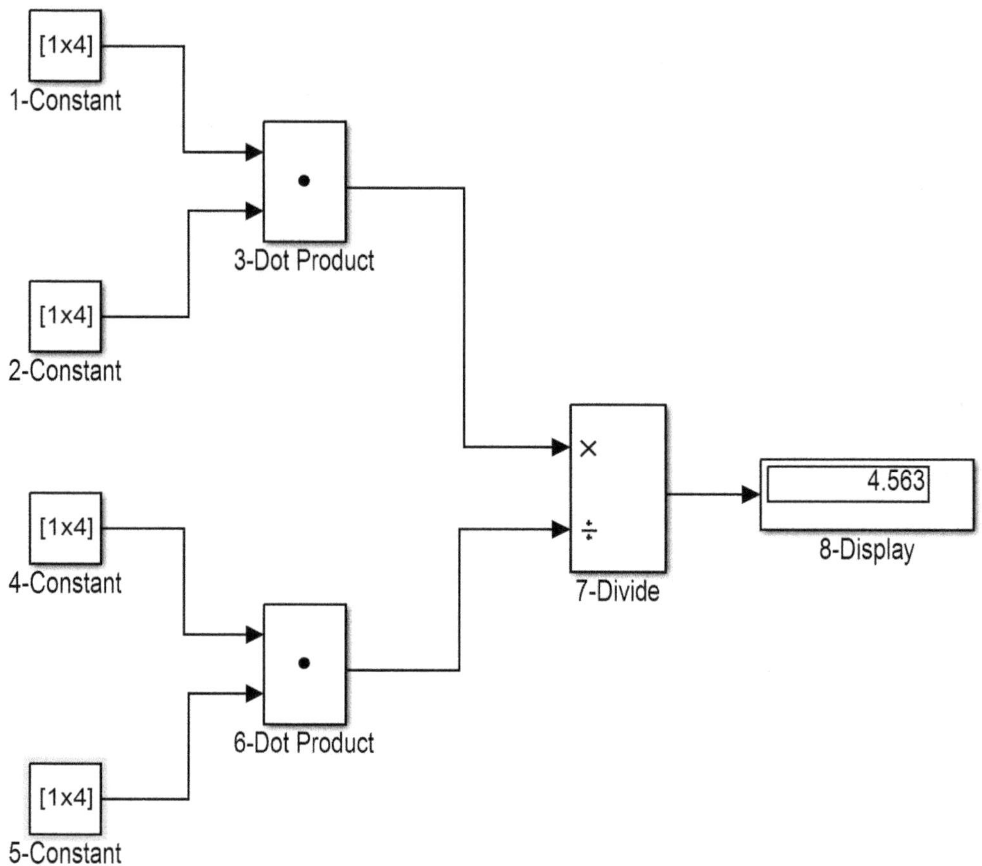

Figure 3.4 Simulink model for dot product

Details of blocks are given in Table 3.4.

Table 3.4 Details of blocks - Dot product

Name of block in model	Name of block in Simulink library	Source	Properties
1-Constant	Constant	Commonly used blocks	Constant value: [3 7 1 9]
2-Constant	Constant	Commonly used blocks	Constant value: [5 2 8 4]
3-Dot product	Dot product	Math operations	---
4-Constant	Constant	Commonly used blocks	Constant value: [1 3 1 2]
5-Constant	Constant	Commonly used blocks	Constant value: [2 1 3 4]
6-Dot product	Dot product	Math operations	---
7-Divide	Divide	Math operations	---
8-Display	Display	Sinks	---

Alternatively same can be obtained using the simulink model shown in Figure 3.5.

Figure 3.5 Simulink model for dot product using matlab function

Details of blocks are given in Table 3.5.

Table 3.5 Details of blocks - Dot product using matlab function

Name of block in model	Name of block in Simulink library	Source	Properties
1-Constant	Constant	Commonly used blocks	Constant value: [3 7 1 9; 5 2 8 4; 1 3 1 2; 2 1 3 4]

2-MATLAB Function	MATLAB Function	User-defined functions	The following code needs to be entered & saved in resulting function file:
			function y = prodsumdivid(u)
			y1=u(1,1)*u(2,1)+u(1,2)*u(2,2)+u(1,3)*u(2,3)+u(1,4)*u(2,4);
			y2=u(3,1)*u(4,1)+u(3,2)*u(4,2)+u(3,3)*u(4,3)+u(3,4)*u(4,4);
			y = y1/y2;

3-Display	Display	Sinks	---

3.3 DETERMINANT OF MATRICES

Determinant can be evaluated for square matrices. Determinant of a simple 2x2 matrix is subtraction of product of primary diagonal elements and secondary diagonal elements.

EXAMPLE 3.3

To build Simulink models for performing following matrix operations:

(*i*) Find determinants of A $= \begin{bmatrix} 2 & 7 & 6 \\ 4 & 9 & 3 \\ 1 & 5 & 2 \end{bmatrix}$ and B

$= \begin{bmatrix} 1 & 0 & 0 \\ 0 & 1 & 0 \\ 0 & 0 & 0 \end{bmatrix}$ and display '1' if both det(A) and det (B) are

non zero numbers otherwise display '0'

(ii)   Find determinants of C $=\begin{bmatrix} 3\ 2\ 5 \\ 7\ 1\ 6 \\ 8\ 4\ 3 \end{bmatrix}$ and D

$=\begin{bmatrix} 1\ 0\ 0 \\ 0\ 1\ 0 \\ 0\ 0\ 0 \end{bmatrix}$ and display '1' if out of det(A) and det (B) atleast one is

non zero number otherwise display '0'

(iii) Compare the results of (i) &

(ii)   and display '1' if atleast anyone of them is zero otherwise display '0'

Simulink model is shown in Figure 3.6.

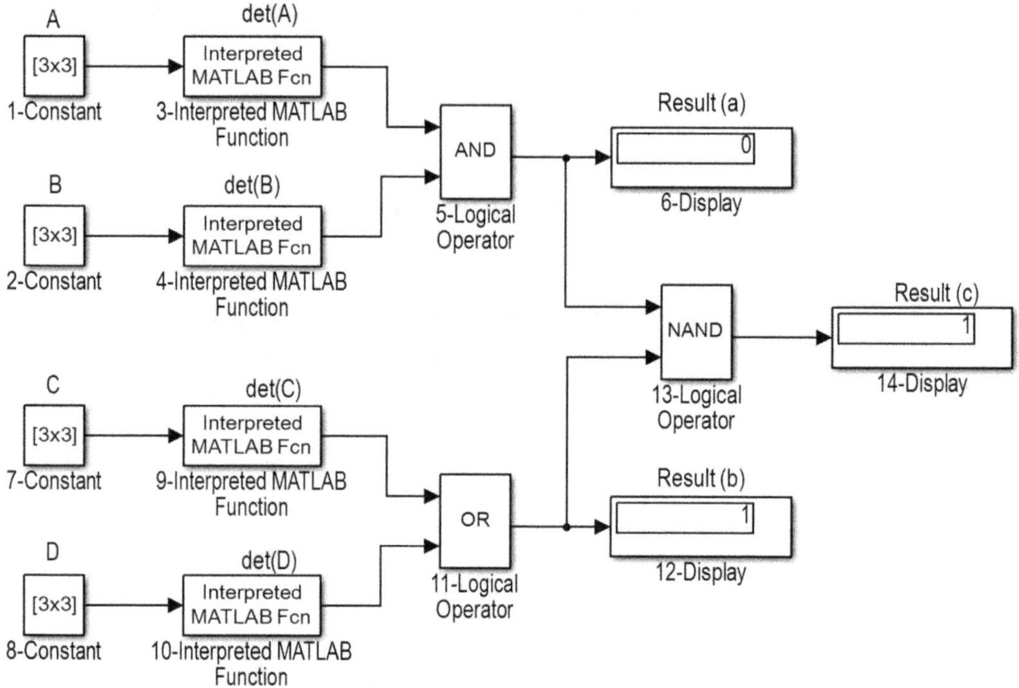

Figure 3.6 Simulink model for determinant of matrix

Details of blocks are given in Table 3.6.

Table 3.6 Details of blocks - Determinant of matrix

Name of block in model	Name of block in Simulink library	Source	Properties
1-Constant	Constant	Commonly used blocks	Constant value: [2 7 6; 4 9 3; 1 5 2]
2-Constant	Constant	Commonly used blocks	Constant value: [1 0 0; 0 1 0; 0 0 0]

Table 3.6 Contd...

Name of block in model	Name of block in Simulink library	Source	Properties
3-Interpreted MATLAB Function	Interpreted MATLAB Function	User-defined functions	MATLAB function: det
4-Interpreted MATLAB Function	Interpreted MATLAB Function	User-defined functions	MATLAB function: det
5-Logical operator	Logical operator	Commonly used blocks	Operator: AND
6-Display	Display	Sinks	----
7-Constant	Constant	Commonly used blocks	Constant value: [3 2 5; 7 1 6; 8 4 3]
8-Constant	Constant	Commonly used blocks	Constant value: [1 0 0; 0 1 0; 0 0 0]
9-Interpreted MATLAB Function	Interpreted MATLAB Function	User-defined functions	MATLAB function: det
10-Interpreted MATLAB Function	Interpreted MATLAB Function	User-defined functions	MATLAB function: det
11-Logical operator	Logical operator	Commonly used blocks	Operator: OR
12-Display	Display	Sinks	----
13-Logical operator	Logical operator	Commonly used blocks	Operator: NAND
14-Display	Display	Sinks	----

Result of using various operators is given in Table 3.7.

Table 3.7 Outcome of various logical operators

Outcome will be 1 if the stated condition is satisfied otherwise 0	
Name of operator	**Condition**
AND	If all inputs are nonzero
OR	If at least one input is nonzero
NAND	If at least one input is zero
NOR	When no inputs are nonzero
XOR	If an odd number of inputs are nonzero
NOT	If the input is zero and vice-versa

Note: Number of inputs can be > 1 for all the operators except for NOT operator

3.4 MATRIX OPERATIONS (SELECTIVE DISPLAY OF ELEMENTS)

Simulink can be extensively used for selective display of elements from a matrix by specifying certain conditions. Results will be displayed according to the conditions specified. These operations will be extremely useful while handling complex mathematical problems.

EXAMPLE 3.4

Given a matrix

$$A = \begin{bmatrix} 11 & 12 & 12 & 14 \\ 21 & 22 & 23 & 24 \\ 21 & 32 & 22 & 34 \\ 41 & 42 & 43 & 44 \end{bmatrix}$$

To build a Simulink model

I.   For evaluating D=B./C where

$$B = \begin{bmatrix} A(2,2) & A(2,4) \\ A(4,2) & A(4,4) \end{bmatrix} \quad C = \begin{bmatrix} A(1,1) & A(1,3) \\ A(3,1) & A(3,3) \end{bmatrix}$$

II. Evaluate determinant of matrix D then display matrix C if det(D) = 0 and display matrix B if det(D) = 1

The following blocks are used to build the model.

I.   **Selector** block is used to extract matrix C and matrix D from matrix A, further **divide** block is used to evaluate matrix D

II. **Interpreted MATLAB function** block is used to find determinant of matrix D. **Index vector** block is used to display matrix B or matrix C depending on the value of determinant of matrix D.

Associated Simulink model (After running the simulation) is shown in Figure 3.7.

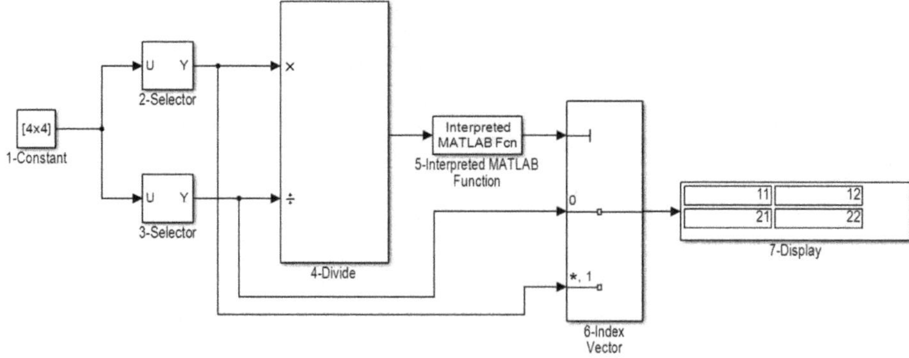

Figure 3.7 Simulink model for selective display of elements

Depending on the index values defined in the function block parameters window of **selector** block, elements from matrix A will be extracted. Specifying [2 4] in index 1 indicates the row numbers and [2 4] in index 2 indicates the column numbers.

Details of blocks are given in Table 3.8.

Table 3.8 Details of blocks - Selective display of elements

Name of block in model	Name of block in Simulink library	Source	Properties
1-Constant	Constant	Commonly used blocks	Constant value: [11 12 12 14; 21 22 23 24; 21 32 22 34; 41 42 43 44]
2-Selector	Selector	Signal routing	Index 1: [2 4] Index 2: [2 4]
3-Selector	Selector	Signal routing	Index 1: [1 3] Index 2: [1 3]
4-Divide	Divide	Math operations	---
5-Interpreted MATLAB Function	Interpreted MATLAB Function	User-defined functions	MATLAB function: det
6-Index vector	Index vector	Index vector	Number of data ports: 2
7-Display	Display	Sinks	---

Note: First signal of **index vector** block is known as control signal. Other signals are known as input data signals. In this example **index vector** block has 2 input data signals. They will be considered as 0, 1, etc., if 'data signal order' in function block parameters is set to be 'zero-based contiguous' (Which is default) and the same will be considered as 1, 2, etc., if 'data signal order' in function block parameters is set to be 'one-based contiguous'. If control signal receives '0' as input then data connected to first input data signal will be displayed in **display** block or if control signal receives '1' as input then data connected to second input data signal will be displayed in **display** block.

EXAMPLE 3.5

To build Simulink model for evaluating the inverse of

$$\begin{bmatrix} 34 & 53 & 20 \\ 42 & 74 & 61 \\ 73 & 28 & 90 \end{bmatrix}$$

And then display

Positive numbers only from result and rest all as 0

Negative numbers only from result and rest all as 0

Inverse is performed in **constant** block itself. For displaying positive numbers only from result, **MinMax Running Resettable** block is used with function as **max** and for displaying rest all as 0, initial condition in this block is set as 0. Whereas for displaying negative numbers only from result, same block with function as **min** is used while setting 0 for initial condition.

Associated Simulink model is shown in Figure 3.8.

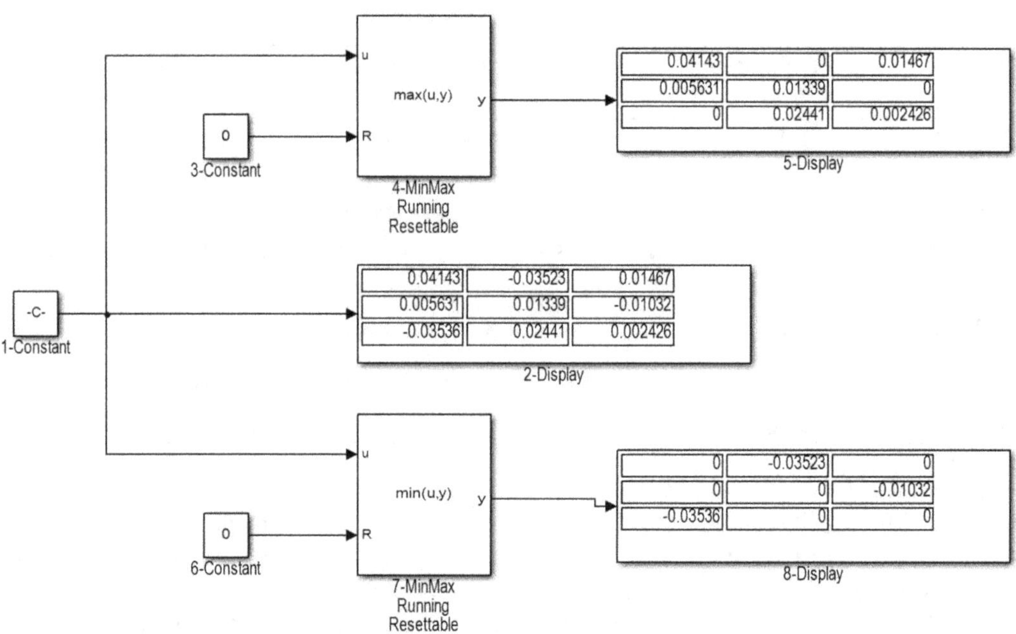

Figure 3.8 Simulink model for performing matrix inverse

Details of blocks are given in Table 3.9.

Table 3.9 Details of blocks - Matrix inverse

Name of block in model	Name of block in Simulink library	Source	Properties
1-Constant	Constant	Commonly used blocks	Constant value: inv([34 53 20; 42 74 61; 73 28 90])
2-Display	Display	Sinks	---

Name of block in model	Name of block in Simulink library	Source	Properties
3-Constant	Constant	Commonly used blocks	Constant value: 0
4-MinMax Running Resettable	MinMax Running Resettable	Math operations	Function: max Initial condition: 0
5-Display	Display	Sinks	---
6-Constant	Constant	Commonly used blocks	Constant value: 0
7-MinMax Running Resettable	MinMax Running Resettable	Math operations	Function: min Initial condition: 0
8-Display	Display	Sinks	---

***Note:* Display** blocks needs to be dragged to sufficient extent for displaying the results. Initial condition can be any value and same will be displayed.

EXAMPLE 3.6

To build Simulink model for evaluating magnitude, reciprocal, conjugate, transpose and hermitian for the following matrix.

$$\begin{bmatrix} 4+5i & 7-9i \\ 3+2i & -3+6i \end{bmatrix}$$

Magnitude will be evaluated as follows:

$$\begin{bmatrix} 4^2+5^2 & 7^2+9^2 \\ 3^2+2^2 & 3^2+6^2 \end{bmatrix}$$

Reciprocal = 1/Matrix

Hermitian = Complex conjugate transpose

This can be achieved by **Math function** block. Associated Simulink model is shown in Figure 3.9.

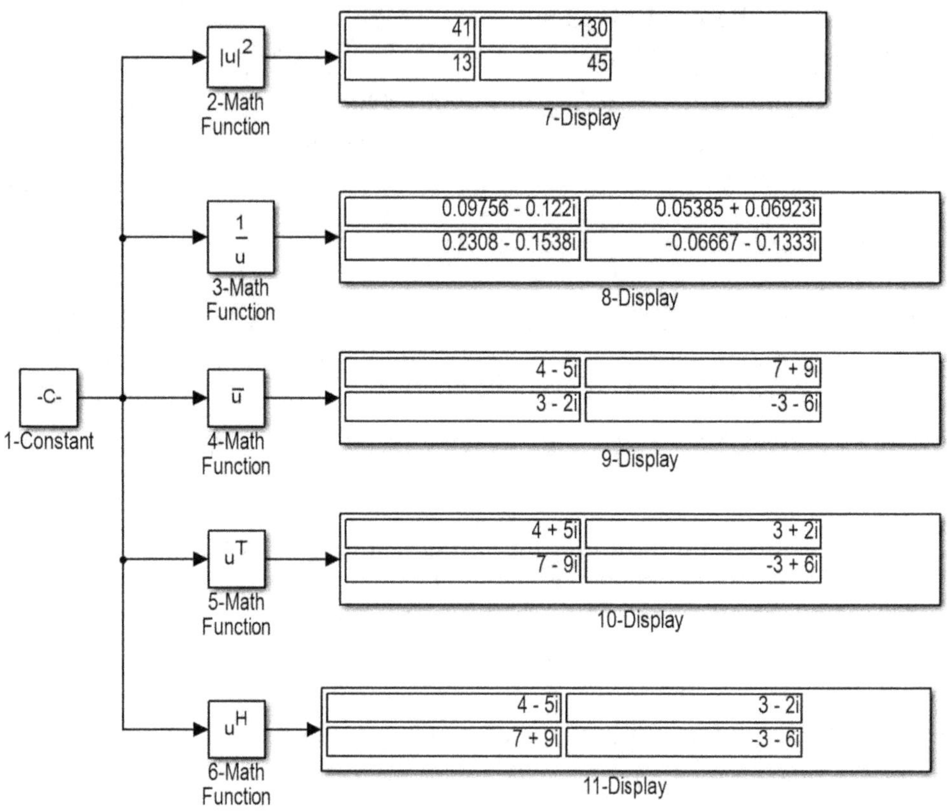

Figure 3.9 Simulink model for performing matrix operations

Details of blocks are given in Table 3.10.

Table 3.10 Details of blocks - Matrix operations

Name of block in model	Name of block in Simulink library	Source	Properties
1-Constant	Constant	Commonly used blocks	Constant value: [4+5i 7-9i; 3+2i -3+6i]
2-Math function	Math function	Math operations	Function: Magnitude^2
3-Math function	Math function	Math operations	Function: Reciprocal
4-Math function	Math function	Math operations	Function: Conj
5-Math function	Math function	Math operations	Function: Transpose
6-Math function	Math function	Math operations	Function: Hermitian
7,8,9,10&11-Display	Display	Sinks	---

Note: **Display** blocks needs to be dragged to sufficient extent for displaying the results.

EXAMPLE 3.7

Given A = [1]; B = [2]

To build Simulink model for

(i) Assembling A & B into row vector C
(ii) Transform vector C to column vector D
(iii) Assembling A & B into column vector E
(iv) Assembling D & E into column vector F
(v) Assembling D & E into matrix G
(vi) Assigning 1000 to element corresponding to 2nd row and 1st column position in matrix G

For accomplishing the above, the following blocks are used

(i) **Matrix concatenate** block is used while choosing concatenate dimension as 2 (Clubbing column wise)

(ii) **Reshape** block is used by choosing output dimensionality option as column vector 2-D (For transforming row vector to column vector)

(iii) **Matrix concatenate** block is used while choosing concatenate dimension as 1 (Clubbing row wise)

(iv) **Vector concatenate** block is used while choosing mode option as vector to assemble as a single column vector

(v) **Vector concatenate** block is used while choosing mode option as multidimensional array and concatenate dimension as 2 so as to assemble column after column to get a matrix

(vi) **Assignment** block is used with the following options

Number of output dimensions: 2 (If it is 1 row indexing only can be done)

Index mode: Zero-based (Usual representation of Simulink wherein indexing i.e. counting of rows and columns starts from 0)

1 Index vector: 1 (2nd row)

2 Index vector: 0 (1st column)

for assigning 1000 to 2nd row and 1st column position in matrix G

Associated Simulink model is shown in Figure 3.10.

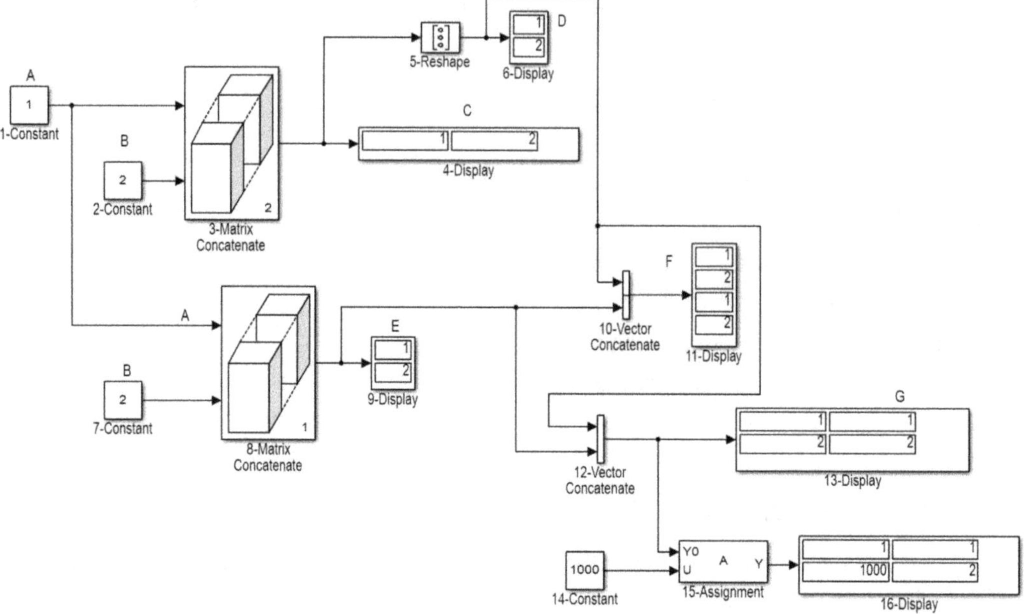

Figure 3.10 Simulink model for assembling sub matrices

Details of blocks are given in Table 3.11.

Table 3.11 Details of blocks - Assembling sub matrices

Name of block in model	Name of block in Simulink library	Source	Properties
1-Constant	Constant	Commonly used blocks	Constant value: 1
2-Constant	Constant	Commonly used blocks	Constant value: 2
3-Matrix concatenate	Matrix concatenate	Math operations	Concatenate dimension: 2
4-Display	Display	Sinks	---
5-Reshape	Reshape	Math operations	Output dimensionality: Column vector (2-D)
6-Display	Display	Sinks	---
7-Constant	Constant	Commonly used blocks	Constant value: 2
8-Matrix concatenate	Matrix concatenate	Math operations	Mode: Multidimensional array Concatenate dimension: 1
9-Display	Display	Sinks	---
10-Vector concatenate	Vector concatenate	Math operations	Mode: Vector

Name of block in model	Name of block in Simulink library	Source	Properties
11-Display	Display	Sinks	---
12-Vector concatenate	Vector concatenate	Math operations	Mode: Multidimensional array Concatenate dimension: 2
13-Display	Display	Sinks	---
14-Constant	Constant	Commonly used blocks	Constant value: 1000
15-Assignment	Assignment	Math operations	Number of output dimensions: 2 Index mode: Zero-based Index (1): 1 Index (2): 0
16-Display	Display	Sinks	---

3.5 SUMMARY

Extensive use of Simulink for handling various matrix operations is presented. Starting from basic operations like matrix multiplication, dot product, inverse of matrix, determinant, etc. it extended up to assembling and assignment level of operations. Further models are built for computation of magnitude, reciprocal, conjugate, transpose and hermitian.

CHAPTER 4

Algebraic Equations

4.0 ALGEBRAIC EQUATIONS

Dealing with algebraic equations is inevitable while working in the domain of mathematics. To commence with solving complex algebraic equation will be the first door step. Further evaluating these equations in various forms starting from polynomial and displaying results while satisfying certain conditions is order of the day. Simulink offers various features to meet the above mentioned needs. This chapter brings out features of Simulink with respect to mathematical treatment of algebraic equations.

4.1 SOLVING ALGEBRAIC EQUATION

Aid of software tools will be needed for solving algebraic equations of higher order in particular. Following examples illustrate implementation of Simulink for doing so.

EXAMPLE 4.1

To build Simulink model for solving

$$4x^3-5x^2+7x-2 = 0$$

Algebraic constraint block is used to solve the equation. It takes initial guess as input, limits the equation to 0 and solves the equation. It ensures that for the final value of x equation is satisfied i.e. equal to 0.

Associated Simulink model is shown in Figure 4.1.

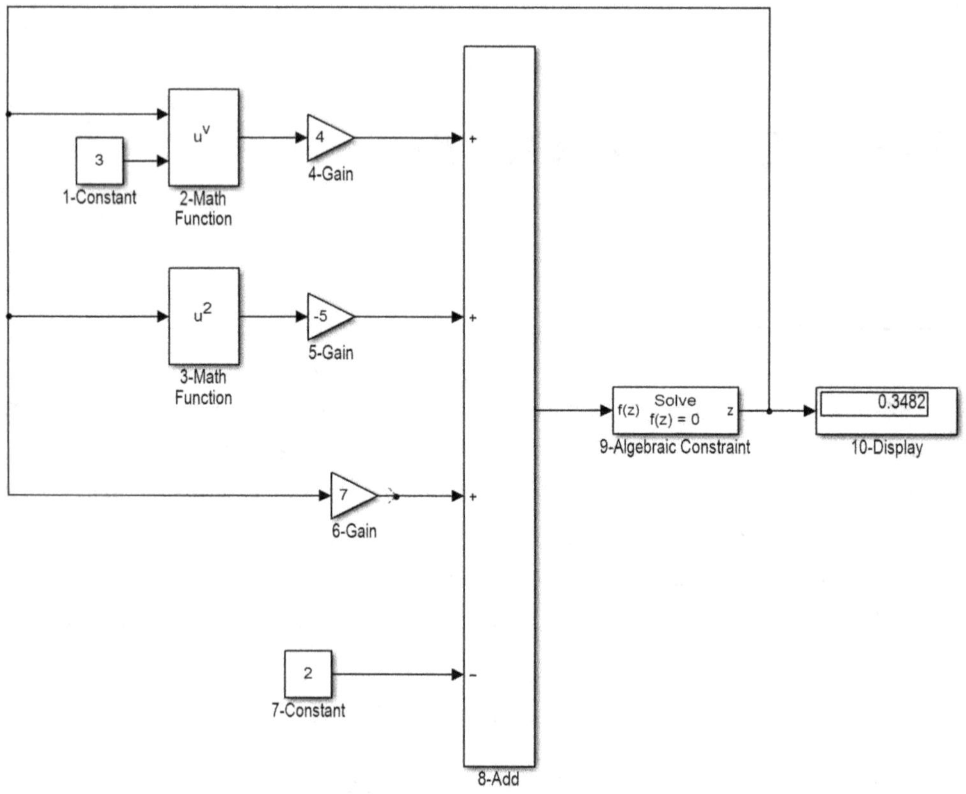

Figure 4.1 Simulink model for solving algebraic equation

Details of blocks are given in Table 4.1.

Table 4.1 Details of blocks - Solving algebraic equation

Name of block in model	Name of block in Simulink library	Source	Properties
1-Constant	Constant	Commonly used blocks	Constant value: 3
2-Math function	Math function	Math operations	Function: pow
3-Math function	Math function	Math operations	Function: square
4-Gain	Gain	Commonly used blocks	Gain: 4
5-Gain	Gain	Commonly used blocks	Gain: -5
6-Gain	Gain	Commonly used blocks	Gain: 7
7-Constant	Constant	Commonly used blocks	Constant value: 2
8-Add	Add	Math operations	List of signs: +++-
9-Algebraic constraint	Algebraic constraint	Math operations	Initial guess: 1
10-Display	Display	Sinks	----

4.2 EVALUATING POLYNOMIAL

Worked out examples are presented for evaluating polynomial and displaying results while satisfying the necessary conditions. These examples are exhaustive with respect to competence of Simulink in handling polynomials.

EXAMPLE 4.2

To build Simulink model for evaluating the polynomial $5x^3+3x^2+2x+1$ for x = 2.5 and display the result with following rounding options

Without rounding (b) Rounding to the nearest number towards zero (c) Rounding to nearest number $5x^3+3x^2+2x+1$ for x = -2.5 and display the result with following rounding options

Without rounding (b) Rounding to the nearest number towards $-\infty$ (c) Rounding to the nearest number towards $+\infty$

Polynomial block is used to feed the given polynomial by specifying numbers which are coefficients of polynomial starting from higher order. **Rounding function** block is implemented with various options to display the results in desired forms. **Fix** option is used to round the result to nearest number towards zero. **Round** option is used to round the result to nearest number. **Floor** option is used to round the result to nearest number towards $-\infty$. **Ceil** option is used to round the result to nearest number towards $+\infty$.

Associated Simulink model is shown in Figure 4.2.

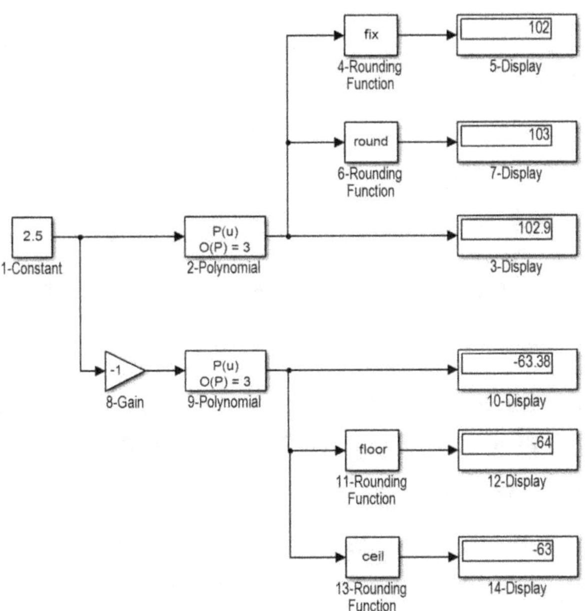

Figure 4.2 Simulink model for evaluating polynomial

Details of blocks are given in Table 4.2.

Table 4.2 Details of blocks - Evaluating polynomial

Name of block in model	Name of block in Simulink library	Source	Properties
1-Constant	Constant	Commonly used blocks	Constant value: 2.5
2-Poynomial	Polynomial	Math operations	Polynomial coefficients: [5 3 2 1]
3-Display	Display	Sinks	----
4-Rounding function	Rounding function	Math operations	Function: fix
5-Display	Display	Sinks	----
6-Rounding function	Rounding function	Math operations	Function: round
7-Display	Display	Sinks	----
8-Gain	Gain	Commonly used blocks	Gain: -1
9-Poynomial	Polynomial	Math operations	Polynomial coefficients: [5 3 2 1]
10-Display	Display	Sinks	----
11-Rounding function	Rounding function	Math operations	Function: floor
12-Display	Display	Sinks	----
13-Rounding function	Rounding function	Math operations	Function: ceil
14-Display	Display	Sinks	----

Note: **Display** blocks needs to be dragged to sufficient extent for displaying the results.

EXAMPLE 4.3

To build Simulink model for evaluating the following algebraic equations and display '1' if result of first one is greater than or equal to that of second one otherwise display '0'.

$$4x^3-5x^2+3x-3 \text{ and } 3x^3-7x^2+4x+5 \text{ for } x=3$$

Fcn block is used for modeling algebraic equations and relational operator is used for comparing the result. Simulink model is shown in Figure 4.3.

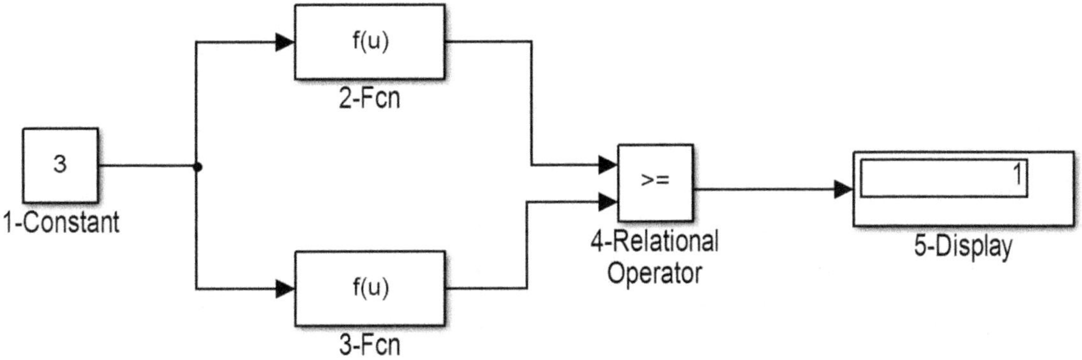

Figure 4.3 Simulink model for evaluating algebraic equations & selective display of result

Details of blocks are given in Table 4.3.

Table 4.3 Details of blocks - Evaluating algebraic equations & for selective display of result

Name of block in model	Name of block in Simulink library	Source	Properties
1-Constant	Constant	Commonly used blocks	Constant value: 3
2-Fcn	Fcn	User-Defined functions	Expression: 4*u^3-5*u^2+3*u-3
3-Fcn	Fcn	User-Defined functions	Expression: 3*u^3-7*u^2+4*u+5
4-Relational operator	Relational operator	Commonly used blocks	Relational operator: >=
5-Display	Display	Sinks	----

Note: If the stated condition in relational operator is satisfied result '1' will be displayed otherwise '0' will be displayed.

Relational operators other than specified in the above problem are '==', '~=', '<', '<=', '>'

EXAMPLE 4.4

To build Simulink models for evaluating the following algebraic equation and check whether the result is > 0.

$$3x^3-7x^2+4x+5 \text{ for } x=3$$

Fcn block is used for modeling algebraic equation. **Compare to zero** block with '>' operator is used. Result will be displayed as '1' if the condition is satisfied otherwise 'o'.

Simulink model is shown in Figure 4.4.

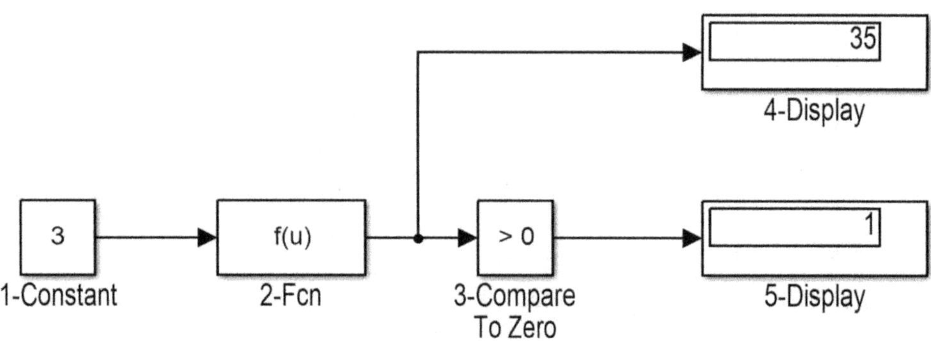

Figure 4.4 Simulink model for evaluating algebraic equation & comparing result with zero

Note: In the above model **5-Display** block displays the final result as '1' as the result after evaluating given algebraic equation satisfies the given condition i.e. 35>0. However **4-Display** block is also used to know the result after evaluating algebraic equation for the sake of understanding.

Details of blocks are given in Table 4.4.

Table 4.4 Details of blocks - Evaluating algebraic equation & comparing result with zero

Name of block in model	Name of block in Simulink library	Source	Properties
1-Constant	Constant	Commonly used blocks	Constant value: 3
2-Fcn	Fcn	User-defined functions	Expression: 3*u^3-7*u^2+4*u+5
3-Compare to zero	Compare to zero	Logic and bit operations	Operator: >
4-Display	Display	Sinks	---
5-Display	Display	Sinks	---

Result of using various operators is given in Table 4.5.

Table 4.5 Outcome of various operators

Result will be 1 if the stated condition is satisfied otherwise 0	
Name of operator	**Condition**
==	Evaluate whether the input is equal to zero
~=	Evaluate whether the input is not equal to zero
<	Evaluate whether the input is less than zero
<=	Evaluate whether the input is less than or equal to zero
>	Evaluate whether the input is more than zero
>=	Evaluate whether the input is more than or equal to zero

EXAMPLE 4.5

To build Simulink model for evaluating the following algebraic equation and check whether the result is < 10.

$$(4x^3-5x^2+3x-3) / (3x^3-7x^2+4x+5) \text{ for } x=4$$

Fcn block is used for modeling algebraic equations. **Compare to constant** block with '<' operator is used. Result will be displayed as '1' if the condition is satisfied otherwise '0' will be displayed.

Simulink model is shown in Figure 4.5.

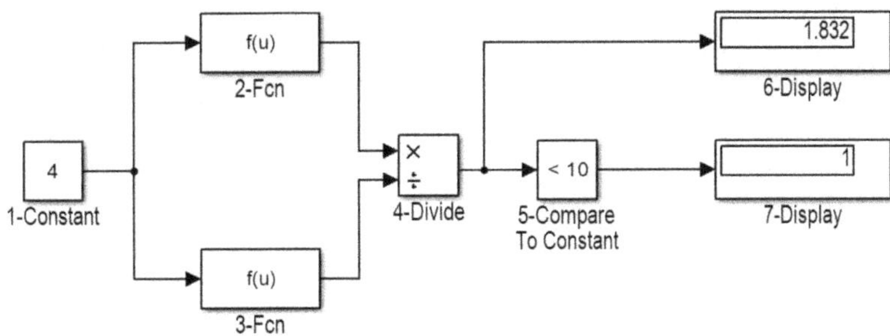

Figure 4.5 Simulink model for evaluating algebraic equation & comparison with constant

Note: In the above model **7-Display** block displays the final result as '1' as the result after evaluating given algebraic equation satisfies the given condition i.e. 1.832<10. However **6-Display** block is also used to know the result after evaluating algebraic equation for the sake of understanding.

Details of blocks are given in Table 4.6.

Table 4.6 Details of blocks - Evaluating algebraic equation and comparison with constant

Name of block in model	Name of block in Simulink library	Source	Properties
1-Constant	Constant	Commonly used blocks	Constant value: 4
2-Fcn	Fcn	User-defined functions	Expression: 4*u^3-5*u^2+3*u-3
3-Fcn	Fcn	User-defined functions	Expression: 3*u^3-7*u^2+4*u+5
4-Divide	Divide	Math operations	---
5-Compare to constant	Compare to constant	Logic and bit operations	Operator: <
6-Display	Display	Sinks	---
7-Display	Display	Sinks	---

Note: Result of using various operators will be same as given in Table 4.5.

4.3 SUMMARY

Methodology to solve algebraic equations using Simulink is presented. Evaluating polynomials and displaying the result of same while satisfying the desired conditions is also discussed. Comparing resulting outcome after evaluating the polynomials with specified constants is elaborated.

CHAPTER 5

Complex Numbers

5.0 COMPLEX NUMBERS

Complex numbers play vital role in evaluating transfer function of various physical quantities. They also have significant role in computing Frequency Response Function (FRF) in characterizing dynamic systems. Methodology to simulate associated operations like addition, polar representation, extraction of real and imaginary parts, computation of absolute quantity, complex conjugate notation, etc in Simulink is elaborated in this chapter.

5.1 ARITHMETIC OPERATION & EXTRACTION OF ABSOLUTE QUANTITY

Absolute quantity of complex numbers needs to be extracted after performing certain arithmetic operations like addition/subtraction. Following example does the same.

EXAMPLE 5.1

To build Simulink model for evaluating the following and display the absolute part of result.

$$\frac{4 + 7i}{6 - 5i} + \frac{3 - 6i}{3 + 2i}$$

This can be achieved by **Abs** block. Associated Simulink model is shown in Figure 5.1.

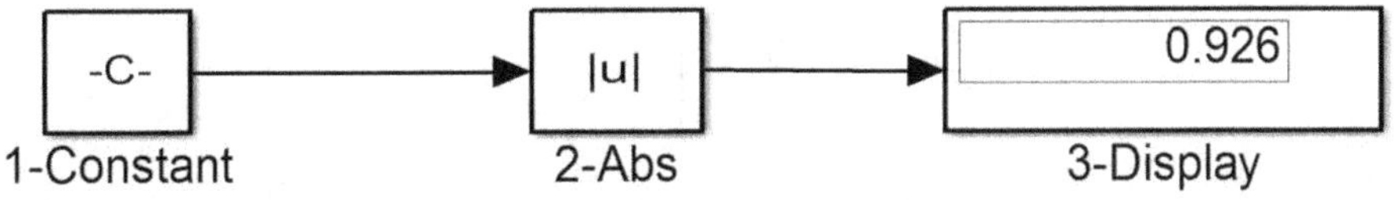

Figure 5.1 Simulink model for performing arithmetic operation of complex numbers

Details of blocks are given in Table 5.1.

Table 5.1 Details of blocks - Performing arithmetic operation of complex numbers

Name of block in model	Name of block in Simulink library	Source	Properties
1-Constant	Constant	Commonly used blocks	Constant value: (4+7i)/(6-5i)+(3-6i)/(3+2i)
2-Abs	Abs	Math operations	---
3-Display	Display	Sinks	---

5.2 MULTIPLICATION OF COMPLEX NUMBER WITH ITS CONJUGATE

Complex number often needs to be multiplied with its conjugate in the process of computing magnitude. Application of Simulink for executing such requirement is demonstrated in the following example.

EXAMPLE 5.2

Given a complex number 9-2i, build a Simulink model to
  (i)   Find the conjugate of same and multiply the complex number with its conjugate
  (ii)   Find the square of given complex number
  (iii) Show the result in one display block upon selection of outcome of either (i) or (ii)

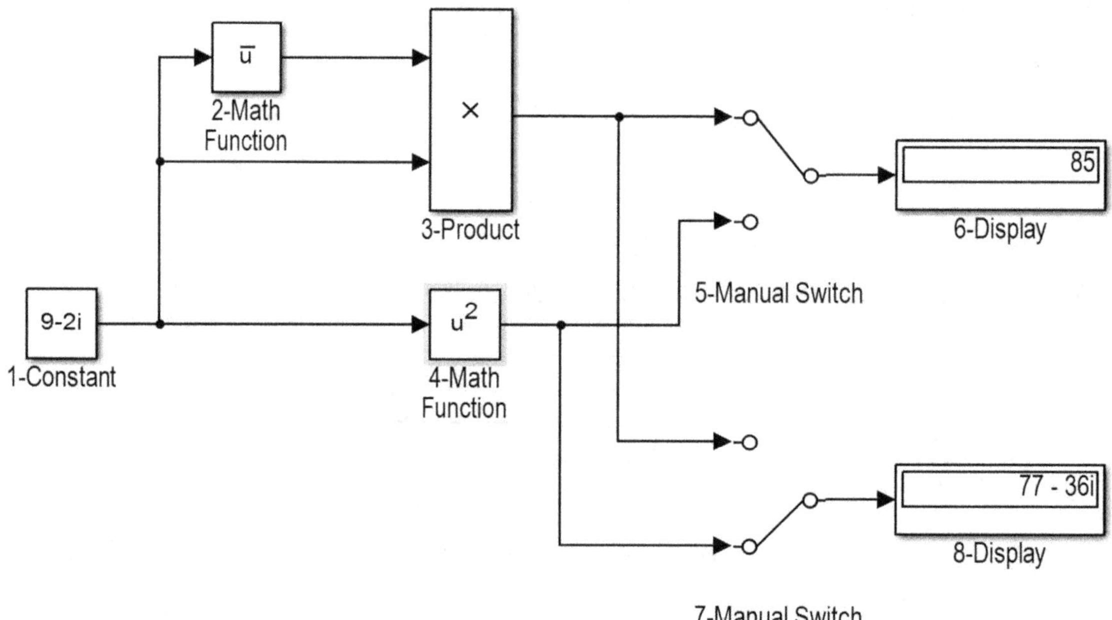

Figure 5.2 Simulink model for multiplication of complex number with its conjugate

The following blocks are used:
  (i)   For evaluating conjugate, **math function** block with **conj** function is used. **Product** block is used to multiply the complex number with its conjugate.
  (ii) **Math function** block with 'square' function is used.
  (iii) Results of (i) and (ii) are connected to two **manual switch** blocks independently. By double clicking this block output will be switched from one input to other input.

Associated Simulink model is shown in Figure 5.2.

Details of blocks are given in Table 5.2.

Table 5.2 Details of blocks - Multiplication of complex number with its conjugate

Name of block in model	Name of block in Simulink library	Source	Properties
1-Constant	Constant	Commonly used blocks	Constant value: 9-2i
2-Math function	Math function	Math operations	Function: conj
3-Product	Product	Commonly used blocks	---
4-Math function	Math function	Math operations	Function: square
5-Manual switch	Manual switch	Signal routing	---
6-Display	Display	Sinks	---
7-Manual switch	Manual switch	Signal routing	---
8-Display	Display	Sinks	---

5.3 COMPLEX TO POLAR NOTATION

Conversion of coordination system from one plane to other plane is a usual requirement in complex mathematics. An example narrating the said conversion is given below.

EXAMPLE 5.3

Given a complex number 8.0375-7.9130i

To build Simulink model for

  (i)   Converting it into polar quantity
  (ii) Convert back the polar quantity thus obtained to complex number
  (iii) Convert the same complex number to real and imaginary parts
  (iv) Convert back the real and imaginary parts thus obtained to complex number

For accomplishing the above, the following blocks are used
  (i)   **Complex to magnitude-angle** block is used for converting the given complex number into polar quantity

(ii) Magnitude-angle to complex block is used for converting back the polar quantity thus obtained to complex number

(iii) Complex to real-imag block is used for converting the same complex number to real and imaginary parts

(iv) Real-imag to complex block is used for converting back the real and imaginary parts thus obtained to complex number.

Associated Simulink model is shown in Figure 5.3.

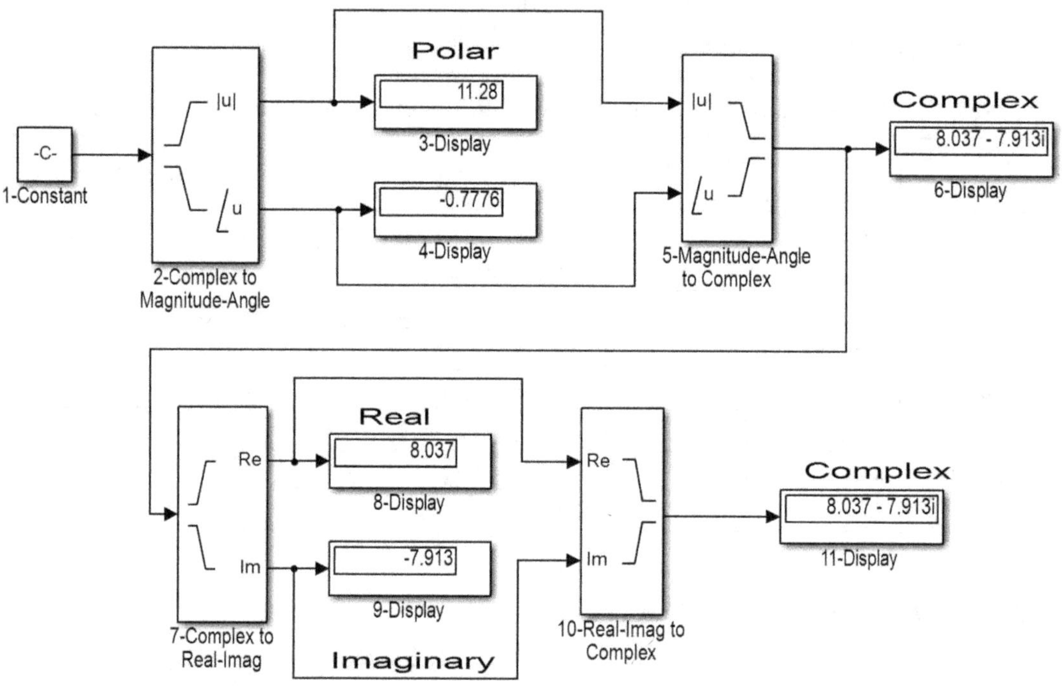

Figure 5.3 Simulink model for converting complex number to polar quantity

Details of blocks are given in Table 5.3.

Table 5.3 Details of blocks - Converting complex number to polar quantity

Name of block in model	Name of block in Simulink library	Source	Properties
1-Constant	Constant	Commonly used blocks	Constant value: 8.0375-7.9130i
2-Complex to magnitude-angle	Complex to magnitude-angle	Math operations	---
3-Display	Display	Sinks	---
4-Display	Display	Sinks	---

Name of block in model	Name of block in Simulink library	Source	Properties
5-Magnitude-angle to complex	Magnitude-angle to complex	Math operations	---
6-Display	Display	Sinks	---
7-Complex to real-imag	Complex to real-imag	Math operations	---
8-Display	Display	Sinks	---
9-Display	Display	Sinks	---
10- Real-imag to Complex	Real-imag to Complex	Math operations	---
11-Display	Display	Sinks	---

5.4 SUMMARY

Mathematical treatment of complex numbers in Simulink is presented. Basic arithmetic operations like addition, subtraction, etc. are dealt with. Computation of absolute quantity for a given complex number is also inclusive. Further multiplication of a complex number with its conjugate is mentioned. Conversion from complex to polar notation is supplementary.

CHAPTER 6

Interpolation and Extrapolation of Data

6.0 INTERPOLATION AND EXTRAPOLATION OF DATA

Statistical means of data processing is an essential practice in many disciplines like census, weather forecast, scientific applications, etc. Interpolation and extrapolation operations are subset of such data processing. Interpolation and extrapolation techniques needs to be adopted due to lack of data at micro intervals. Simulink comes to rescue when operations will be needed for evaluating output data which is function of two sets of input data points. This chapter brings out various modes of interpolation and extrapolation of data using Simulink.

6.1 INTERPOLATION AND EXTRAPOLATION OF 1-D DATA

Interpolation and extrapolation operations using simulink for evaluating output data which is function of one set of input data is a regular requirement. Same is demonstrated using the following example.

EXAMPLE 6.1

Given the data as following:

$$x = [1\ 2\ 3\ 4\ 5]$$

To build Simulink model for evaluating $y = \log_e(x)$ and for displaying values of y for following

$$x = 2 \qquad (ii)\ x = 3.5 \qquad (iii)\ x = 5.5$$

For (i) x = 2, y can be directly taken as x falls within the given data but for other cases it is not direct. For (ii) x=3.5, data needs to be interpolated to find corresponding y and for (iii) x=5.5, data needs to be extrapolated as it is out of range. This can be achieved by 1-D lookup table block.

Associated Simulink model is shown in Figure 6.1.

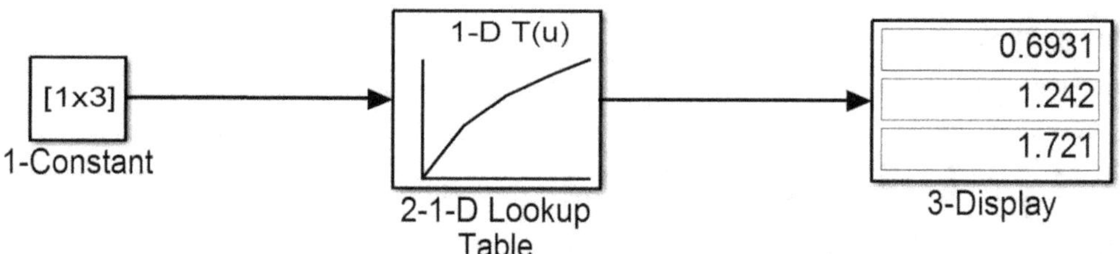

Figure 6.1 Simulink model for data interpolation and extrapolation (1-D)

Details of blocks are given in Table.

Table 6.1 Details of blocks - Data interpolation and extrapolation (1-D)

Name of block in model	Name of block in Simulink library	Source	Properties
1-Constant	Constant	Commonly used blocks	Constant value: [2 3.5 5.5]
2-1-D Lookup table	1-D Lookup table	Lookup tables	Table data: log([1:5]) or Table data: [0 0.6931 1.0986 1.3863 1.6094] Breakpoints 1: [1:5] or Breakpoints 1:[1 2 3 4 5]
3-Display	Display	Sinks	---

6.2   INTERPOLATION AND EXTRAPOLATION OF 1-D DATA (DYNAMIC INPUT)

Sometimes complex requirements such as changing input data while processing for deriving output data will come across. In such instances Simulink can be made use of as can be seen from following example.

EXAMPLE 6.2

Given the following:

$$x = [1\ 2\ 3\ 4\ 5] \text{ and } y = \sin(x) = [0.8414\ 0.9092\ 0.1411\ -0.7568\ -0.9589]$$

To build Simulink model for evaluating y for x = 2.5.

This can be achieved by lookup table dynamic block.

Associated Simulink model is shown in Figure 6.2.

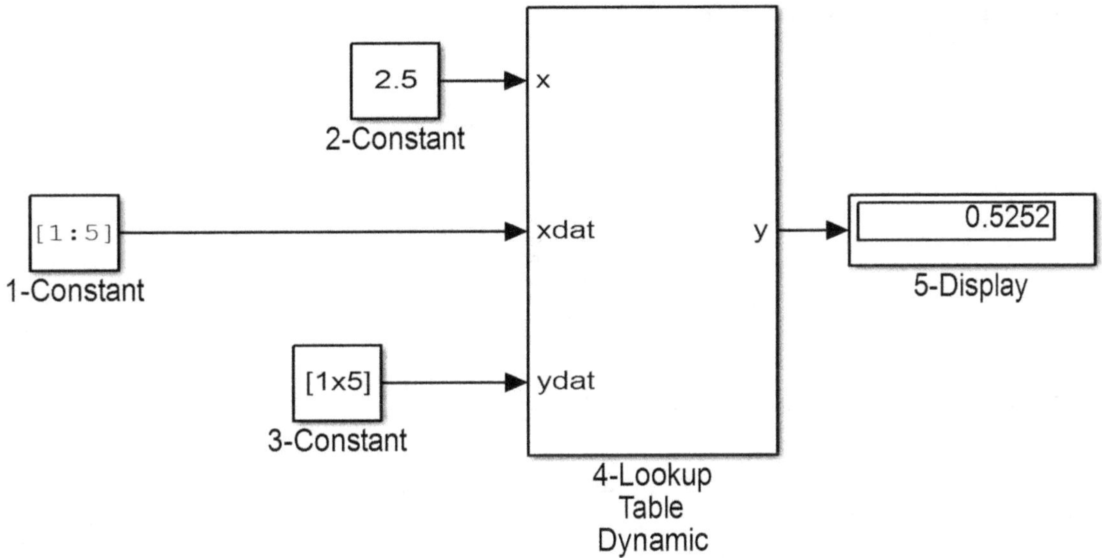

Figure 6.2 Simulink model for displaying index with fraction

Details of blocks are given in Table.

Table 6.2 Details of blocks - Displaying index with fraction

Name of block in model	Name of block in Simulink library	Source	Properties
1-Constant	Constant	Commonly used blocks	Constant value: [1:5]
2-Constant	Constant	Commonly used blocks	Constant value: 2.5
3-Constant	Constant	Commonly used blocks	Constant value: [0.8414 0.9092 0.1411 -0.7568 -0.9589]
4-Lookup table dynamic	Lookup table dynamic	Lookup tables	---
5-Display	Display	Sinks	---

Note: Functionality of lookup table dynamic block is similar to that of other lookup table blocks except one advantage lying with lookup table dynamic block is that the table data can be changed dynamically (Hence the name dynamic) while simulation is running.

6.3   INTERPOLATION AND EXTRAPOLATION OF 2-D DATA

2-D data also needs to be interpolated and extrapolated. Illustration of interpolation and extrapolation of output data which is a function of two sets of input data is given through following example.

EXAMPLE – DATA OPERATIONS FOR 2-D (INTERPOLATION & EXTRAPOLATION)-6.3

Given the data as following:

x	z = x + y		
	y		
	4	5	6
1	5	6	7
2	6	7	8
3	7	8	9

To build Simulink model for evaluating z for (i) x=1 & y=4, (ii) x=2.5 & y=5.5 and (iii) x=3.5 & y=6.5.

For (i) x=1 & y=4, z can be directly taken as x & y falls within the given data but for other cases it is not direct. For (ii) x=2.5 & y=5.5, data needs to be interpolated to find corresponding z and for (iii) x=3.5 & y=6.5, data needs to be extrapolated as it is out of range.

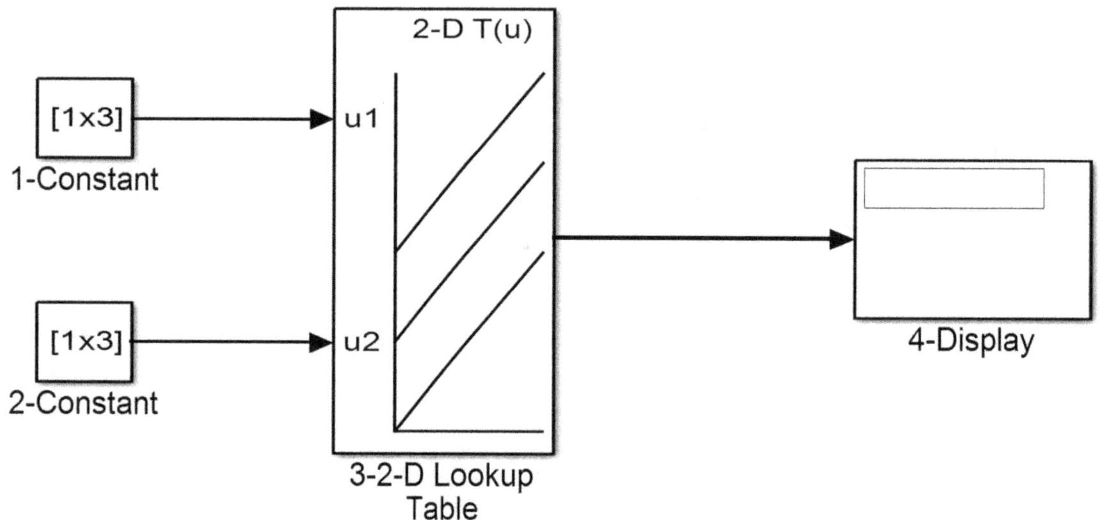

Figure 6.3 Simulink model for data interpolation and extrapolation (2-D)

This can be achieved by 2-D lookup table block.

Associated Simulink model is shown in Figure 6.3.

Details of blocks are given in Table.

Table 6.3 Details of blocks - Data interpolation and extrapolation (2-D)

Name of block in model	Name of block in Simulink library	Source	Properties
1-Constant	Constant	Commonly used blocks	Constant value: [1 2.5 3.5]
2-Constant	Constant	Commonly used blocks	Constant value: [4 5.5 6.5]
3-2-D Lookup table	2-D Lookup table	Lookup tables	Table data: [5 6 7; 6 7 8; 7 8 9] Breakpoints 1: [1 2 3] Breakpoints 2:[4 5 6]
4-Display	Display	Sinks	----

6.4 LOCATING & DISPLAYING ELEMENTS FROM N-D DATA

Simulink models may have to be built for locating and displaying specific elements from n-D (More than 2-D) data also. Approach to be followed in such cases is explained in example given below.

EXAMPLE 6.4

Given the following:

$$\begin{bmatrix} 10 & 20 & 30 & 40 & 50 \\ 11 & 21 & 31 & 41 & 51 \\ 12 & 22 & 32 & 42 & 52 \\ 13 & 23 & 33 & 43 & 53 \\ 14 & 24 & 34 & 44 & 54 \end{bmatrix}$$

To build Simulink model for displaying diagonal elements in the above matrix.

This can be achieved by n-D lookup table block.

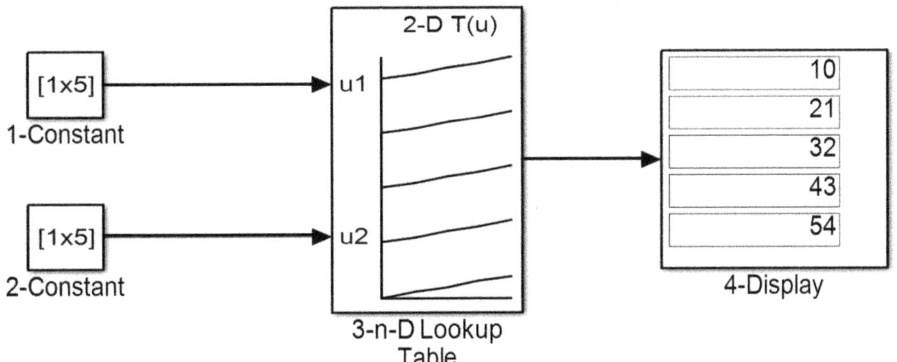

Figure 6.4 Simulink model for locating and displaying specific elements from n-D data

Associated Simulink model is shown in Figure 6.4.

Details of blocks are given in Table 6.4.

Table 6.4 Details of blocks - Locating and displaying specific elements from n-D data

Name of block in model	Name of block in Simulink library	Source	Properties
1-Constant	Constant	Commonly used blocks	Constant value: [1 2 3 4 5]
2-Constant	Constant	Commonly used blocks	Constant value: [1 2 3 4 5]
3-n-D Lookup table	n-D Lookup table	Lookup tables	Table data [10 20 30 40 50; 11 21 31 41 51; 12 22 32 42 52; 13 23 33 43 53; 14 24 34 44 54] Breakpoints 1: [1 2 3 4 5] Breakpoints 2: [1 2 3 4 5]
4-Display	Display	Sinks	---

6.5 DISPLAYING INDEX WITH FRACTION FOR A GIVEN DATA

Simulink offers a promising solution for very specific requirement like displaying index with fraction corresponding to given input data. Following example links to such requirement.

EXAMPLE 6.5

To build Simulink model for displaying index (Position) along with fraction for a given number falling in the given vector.

[2 3 4 5 6]

This can be achieved by pre lookup table block.

Associated Simulink model is shown in Figure 6.5.

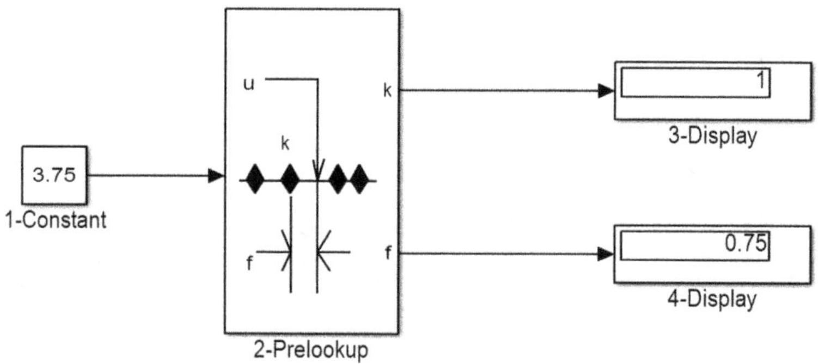

Figure 6.5 Simulink model for displaying index with fraction

3-display block displays '1' as result indicating the index (Position) of the given input data (3.75). This is due to the reason that Simulink starts indexing (Counting) 0,1,2,3,... whereas matlab starts indexing 1,2,3,... Further 4-display block displays '0.75' as result indicating the fraction associated with given input data.

Details of blocks are given in Table 6.5.

Table 6.5 Details of blocks - Displaying index with fraction

Name of block in model	Name of block in Simulink library	Source	Properties
1-Constant	Constant	Commonly used blocks	Constant value: 3.75
2-PreLookup table	Prelookup table	Lookup tables	Breakpoint data: [2 3 4 5 6]
3-Display	Display	Sinks	---
4-Display	Display	Sinks	---

6.6 DATA WRITING, STORING AND READING AT INTERMITTENT INSTANCES

At times it will be required to write, store and read data at specific instances in the path of deriving output data from input data based on given logic. This requirement is complex in nature as same needs to be met without interrupting the chain of input-output.

Method of building a Simulink model to meet the above is given in the following example.

EXAMPLE 6.6

To build a Simulink model for integrating twice a repeating sequence stair signal (With default parameters), write the data at 3 instances i.e. given input data, after integrating first time, after integrating second time and store 3 sets of data and read the same without interrupting main model.

Data store write block is used for writing data, data store memory block is used for storing data and data store read block is used for reading the data.

Associated Simulink model is shown in Figure 6.6.

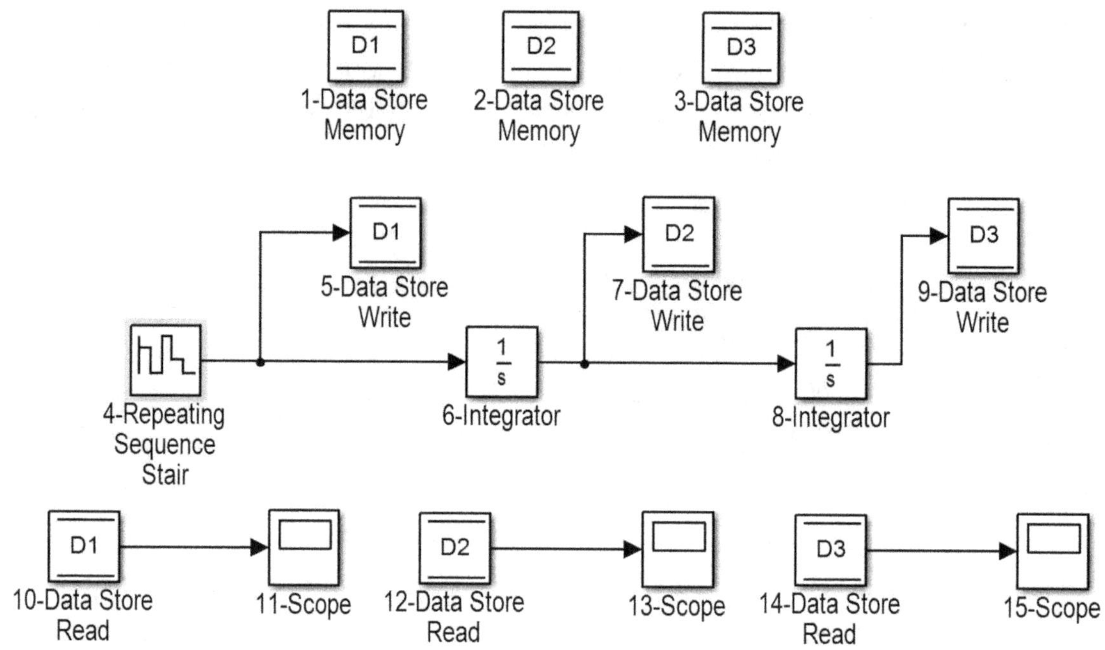

Figure 6.6 Simulink model for writing, storing and reading data

Details of blocks are given in Table 6.6.

Table 6.6 Details of blocks - Writing, storing and reading data

Name of block in model	Name of block in Simulink library	Source	Properties
1-Data store memory	Data store memory	Signal routing	Data store name: D1
2-Data store memory	Data store memory	Signal routing	Data store name: D2
3-Data store memory	Data store memory	Signal routing	Data store name: D3
4-Repeating sequence stair	Repeating sequence stair	Sources	---
5-Data store write	Data store write	Signal routing	Data store name: D1
6-Integrator	Integrator	Continuous	---
7-Data store write	Data store write	Signal routing	Data store name: D2
8-Integrator	Integrator	Continuous	---
9-Data store write	Data store write	Signal routing	Data store name: D3

Name of block in model	Name of block in Simulink library	Source	Properties
10-Data store read	Data store read	Signal routing	Data store name: D1
11-Scope	Scope	Sinks	---
12-Data store read	Data store read	Signal routing	Data store name: D2
13-Scope	Scope	Sinks	---
14-Data store read	Data store read	Signal routing	Data store name: D3
15-Scope	Scope	Sinks	---

Running the model with simulation time of 10 seconds, double clicking 11-scope block, 13-scope block and 15-scope block will generate the plots (After selecting auto scale option) as shown in Figure 6.7 – 6.9 respectively.

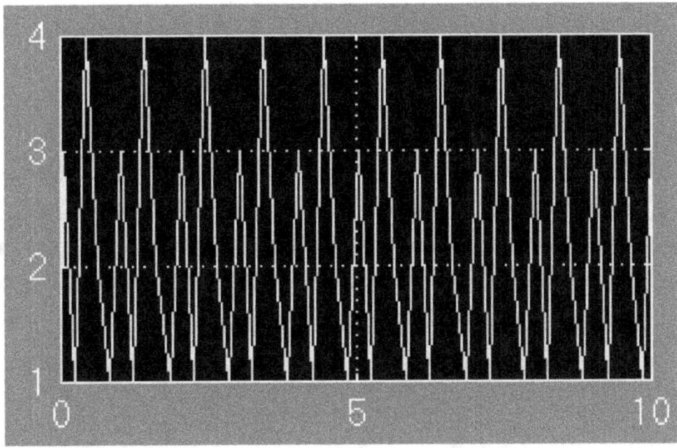

Figure 6.7 Plot corresponding to data read from D1 store memory

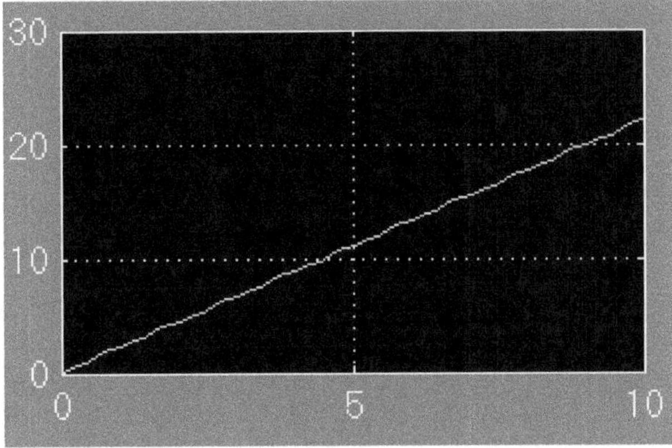

Figure 6.8 Plot corresponding to data read from D2 store memory

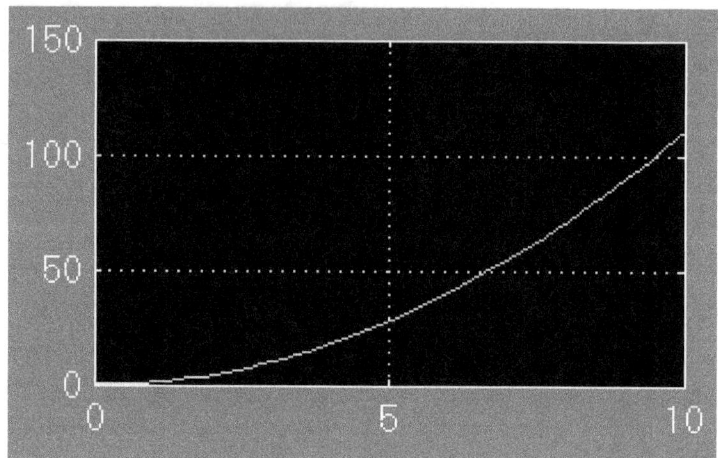

Figure 6.9 Plot corresponding to data read from D3 store memory

6.7 SUMMARY

Interpolation and extrapolation of data for meeting versatile requirements is compiled in this chapter. Implementation of same for 1-D, 2-D and n-D data is shown. Specific requirements like changing input data while it is being processed are addressed. Modeling approach to be followed for locating and displaying specific elements from given input data is presented. Further displaying index from input data corresponding to given number along with fraction with the aid of Simulink is explained. Apart from this means for writing, storing and reading data as and when necessary is also elaborated.

CHAPTER 7

Calculus

7.0 CALCULUS

Differentiation and integration are part of calculus. Both of them are inseparable from real world as they are essentially required to develop mathematical models meant for analyzing physical systems. Performing both differentiation and integration is tedious as such. Hence depending on software tools is inevitable to perform the same. Simulink enables user to handle calculus with utmost ease. This chapter brings out the procedure to deal with differentiation and integration in Simulink.

7.1 DIFFERENTIATION

Basic sense of differentiation is rate of change. Where ever rate of change of certain physical quantities like displacement, velocity, acceleration, etc is needed differentiation comes into play. Following few examples illustrates the methodology to perform differentiation using Simulink.

EXAMPLE 7.1

To build a Simulink model for computing and plotting velocity, acceleration and jerk simultaneously from displacement. Given the following.

Displacement, x = A sin (ωt + ϕ) with A = 1 m, ω = 1 rad/sec, ϕ = 0 rad

Consider a gain of 5.

We know that

$$Velocity = \frac{d}{dt}Displacement \qquad Acceleration = \frac{d}{dt}Velocity \qquad Jerk = \frac{d}{dt}Acceleration$$

Accordingly Derivative block for performing differentiation is needed. To bunch all four parameters to be plotted, bus creator block is used. Further scope block is used for displaying the plots.

Note: Scope block generates plots with yellow, magenta, cyan, red, green, blue in order.

By default bus creator name will be hidden. To enable it select show block name in format option by pressing right mouse button over the block.

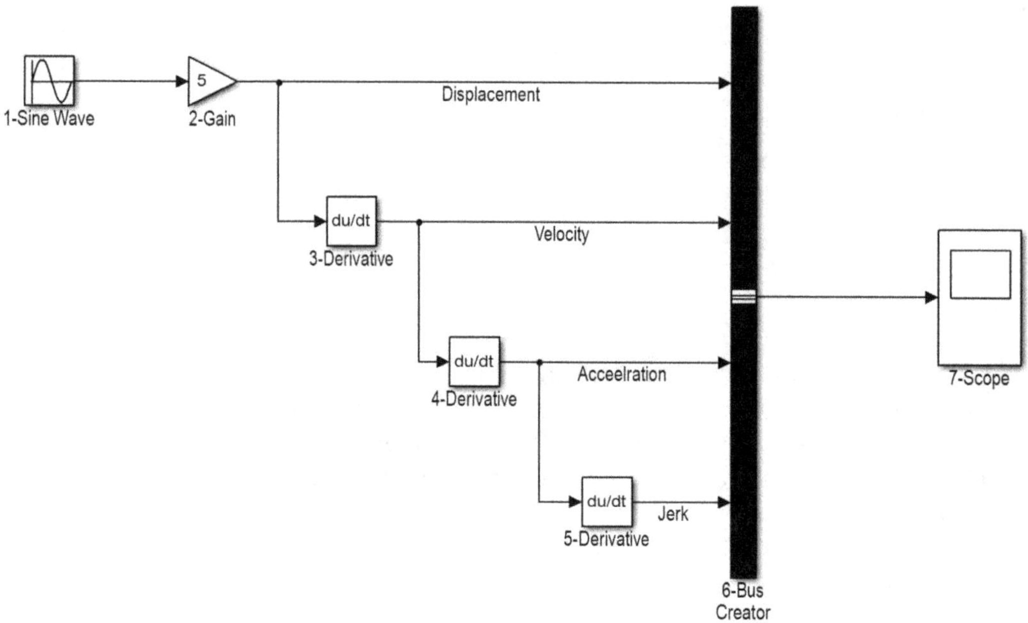

Figure 7.1 Simulink model for computing and plotting velocity, acceleration and jerk

Simulink model is shown in Figure 7.1.

Signals are given labels by double clicking the signal line as shown in Figure. To change the font properties, select signal using left mouse button – right mouse button - format – font style.

Details of blocks are given in Table 7.1.

Table 7.1 Details of blocks - Computing and plotting velocity, acceleration and jerk

Name of block in model	Name of block in Simulink library	Source	Properties
1-Sine wave	Sine wave	Sources	Amplitude: 1 Frequency: 1 Phase: 0
2-Gain	Gain	Commonly used blocks	Gain: 5
3-Derivative	Derivative	Continuous	-----
4-Derivative	Derivative	Continuous	-----
5-Derivative	Derivative	Continuous	-----
6-Bus creator	Bus creator	Commonly used blocks	Number of inputs: 4 Right mouse button – format - Show block name
7-Scope		Sinks	---

Save the model and then run for simulation time of 10 seconds. Scope block needs to be double clicked and then select auto scale option. Ignoring initial spike portion and zooming over sinusoidal portion generates results as shown in Figure 7.2.

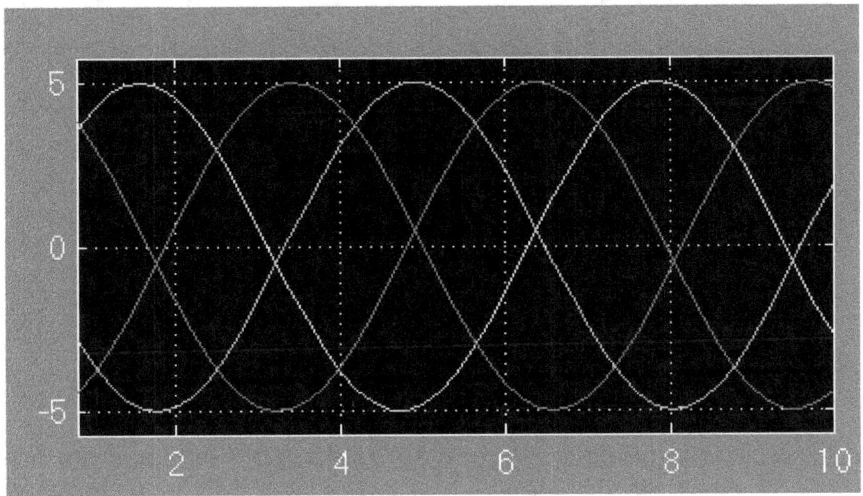

Figure 7.2 Displacement, velocity, acceleration and jerk plots

Note: Yellow, magenta, cyan and red color plots indicate displacement, velocity, acceleration and jerk respectively.

Slider gain block (From math operations) also can be used in place of gain block which facilitates to change the gain while running simulation itself by sliding a bar in the window which appears upon double clicking the slider gain block as shown in Figure 7.3.

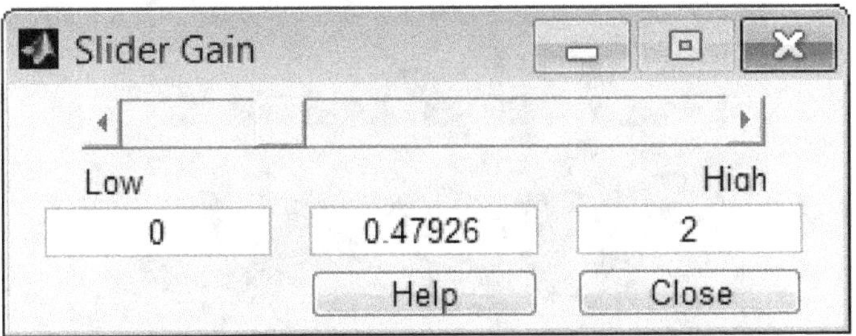

Figure 7.3 Property window – Slider gain block

Further simulink model is reconfigured by replacing Scope block with floating scope block as follows:

Copy the same model and delete bus creator and scope blocks and then position floating scope block (From sinks) in same place as shown in Figure 7.4.

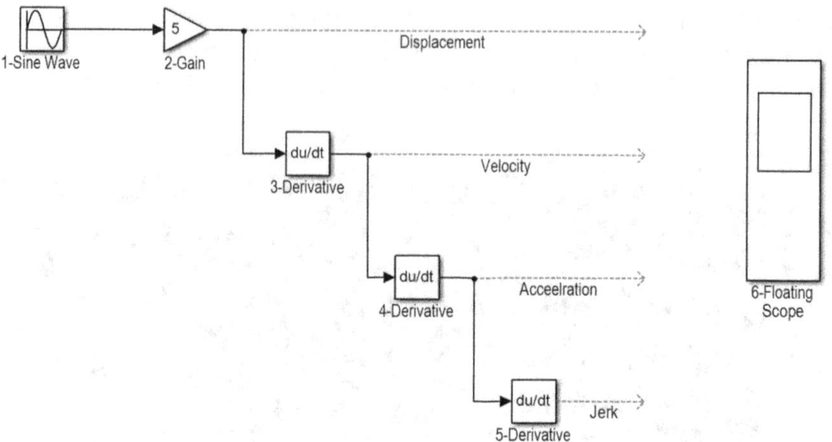

Figure 7.4 Simulink model for computing velocity, acceleration and jerk (With floating scope)

Double click on floating scope block, then select 'parameters' from top and then specify 'number of axes' as 4. The floating scope will take new look as shown in Figure 7.5.

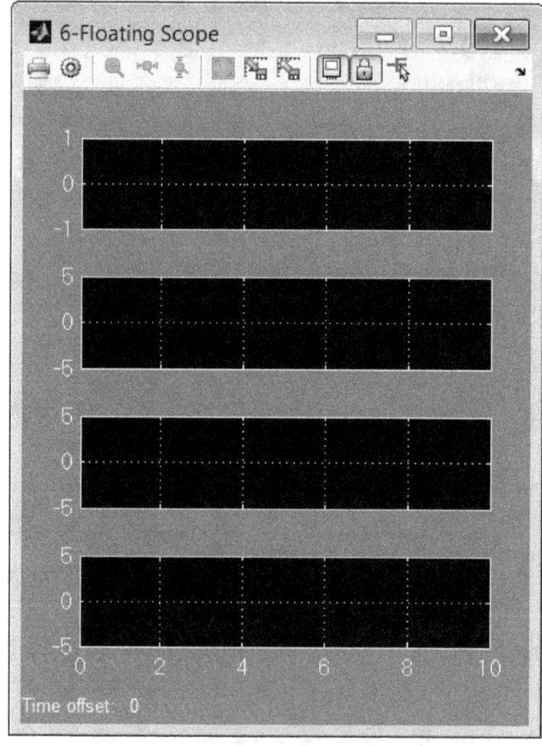

Figure 7.5 Floating scope window

Then select 'model configuration parameters' from top of Simulink model window in which disable 'block reduction'. Then select 'signals and parameters' from LHS of configuration parameters window in which disable 'signal storage reuse' so as to put floating scope in use for simulation. Then to assign the particular data to be displayed in specific part of floating scope, select the first part of floating scope and same will be covered with blue boarder. Then press right mouse button, select signal selection and select 1-sine wave. Repeat the same for rest and select velocity, acceleration and jerk in order. Select first part of floating scope, select right mouse button, select axes properties, specify -1 and 1 for Y-min and Y-max respectively. Running the simulation for 10 seconds, the floating scope window will appear as shown in Figure 7.6.

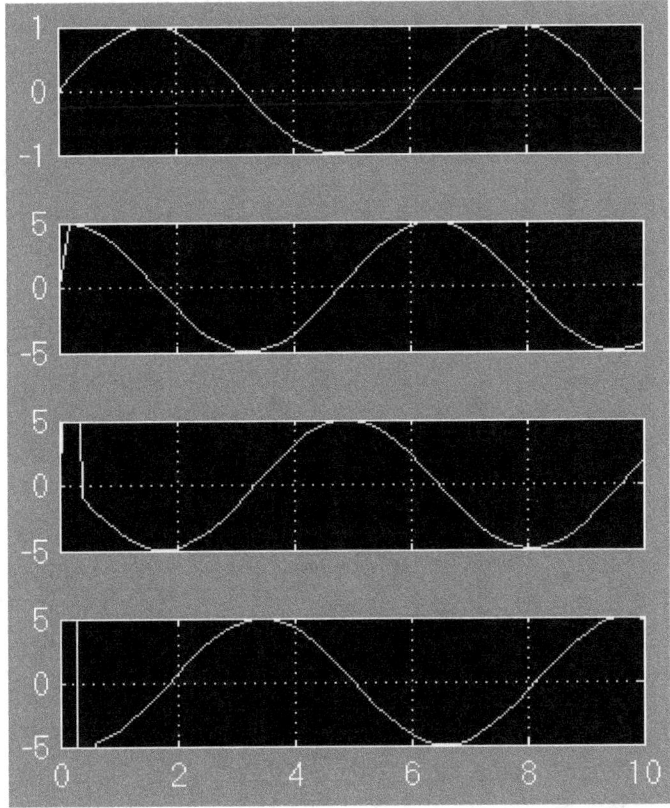

Figure 7.6 Floating scope window with results displayed

EXAMPLE 7.2

To build a Simulink model
(i)   For computing and plotting displacement and velocity simultaneously with following parameters:
Amplitude = 1, Frequency = 0.25 Hz = pi/2 rad/sec

(ii)   Further to replace velocity plot (While retaining displacement plot as it is) with new velocity plot with a scale factor of 0.5 without removing the existing blocks.

The following blocks are used to build the model.
(i)   Sine wave block, derivative block and scope block.
(ii)   Sine wave block, derivative block, Gain block, bus assignment block and scope block.

Associated Simulink model is shown in Figure 7.7.

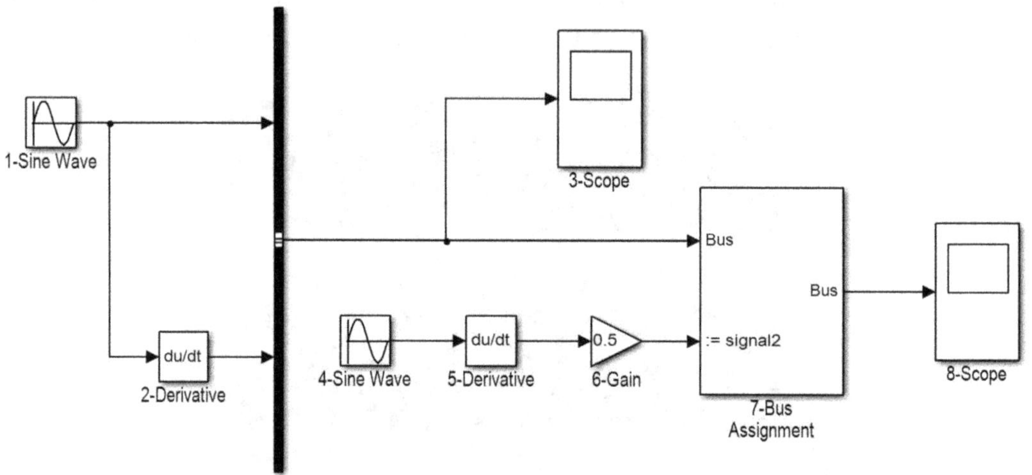

Figure 7.7 Simulink model for plotting displacement and velocity without & with scale factor

Details of blocks are given in Table 7.2.

Table 7.2 Details of blocks - Plotting displacement and velocity without & with scale factor

Name of block in model	Name of block in Simulink library	Source	Properties
1-Sine wave	Sine wave	Sources	Amplitude:1 Frequency: pi/2 rad/sec
2-Derivative	Derivative	Continuous	----
3-Scope	Scope	Sinks	---
4-Sine wave	Sine wave	Sources	Amplitude:1 Frequency: pi/2 rad/sec
5-Derivative	Derivative	Continuous	----
6-Gain	Gain	Commonly used blocks	Gain: 0.5
7-Bus assignment	Bus assignment	Signal routing	Signals that are being assigned: signal1 or signal 2 (Follow note below for details)
8-Scope	Scope	Sinks	---

Note: Bus assignment block will provide the following options:

With signal 1 option placed under signals that are being assigned in block parameters, velocity plot without and with scale factor will be displayed simultaneously in scope (8-Scope).

With signal 2 option, displacement plot and velocity plot with scale factor will be displayed simultaneously in scope (8-Scope).

Running the model with simulation time of 10 seconds, double clicking 3-scope block and then selecting auto scale option, plot shown in Figure 7.8 will be displayed.

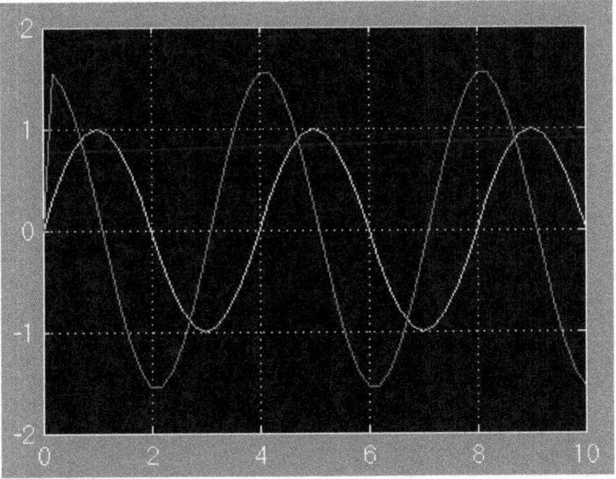

Figure 7.8 Plot of displacement and velocity without scale factor

In the above plot yellow color represents displacement whereas magenta color represents velocity without scale factor.

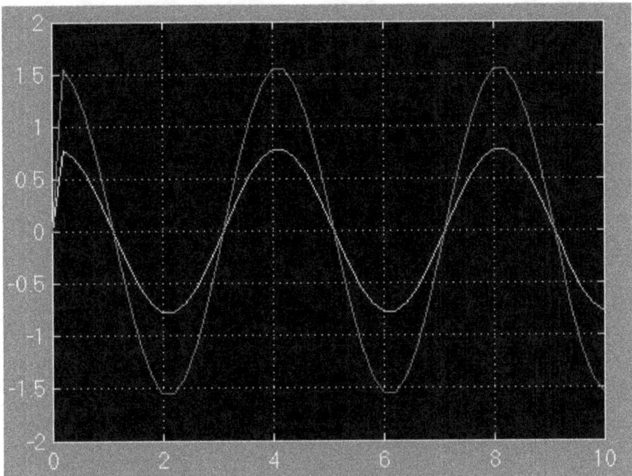

Figure 7.9 Plot of velocity without and with scale factor

With signal 1 option placed under signals that are being assigned in bus assignment block parameters and running the model with simulation time of 10 seconds, double clicking 8-scope block and then selecting auto scale option, plot shown in Figure 7.9 will be displayed.

In the above plot magenta color represents velocity without scale factor whereas yellow color represents velocity with scale factor.

With signal 2 option placed under signals that are being assigned in bus assignment block parameters and running the model with simulation time of 10 seconds, double clicking 8-scope block and then selecting auto scale option, plot shown in Figure 7.10 will be displayed.

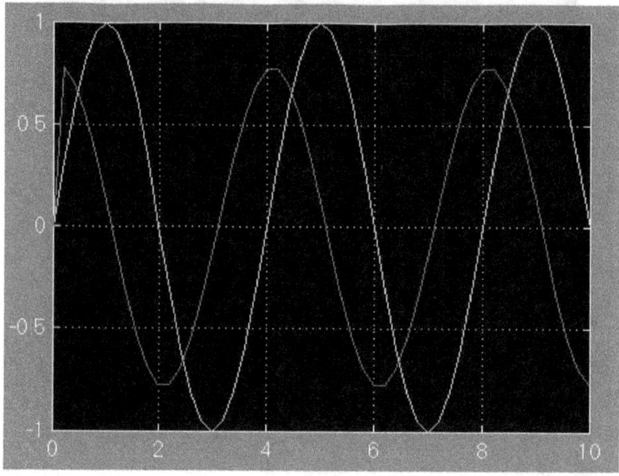

Figure 7.10 Plot of displacement and velocity with scale factor

In the above plot yellow color represents displacement whereas magenta color represents velocity with scale factor.

EXAMPLE 7.3

Given a random signal with following parameters:

Mean: 0; Variance: 1; Sample time: 0.1 sec

Build a Simulink model for plotting first derivative of random signal without connecting signal between input-output blocks

Goto and From blocks are used to transfer data between derivative (Input) and scope (Output) blocks without connecting signals.

Note: One Goto block can transfer data to any number of From blocks but converse is not true.

Goto tag parameter of Goto and From blocks has to be identical. Default parameter is 'A'

Associated Simulink model is shown in Figure 7.11.

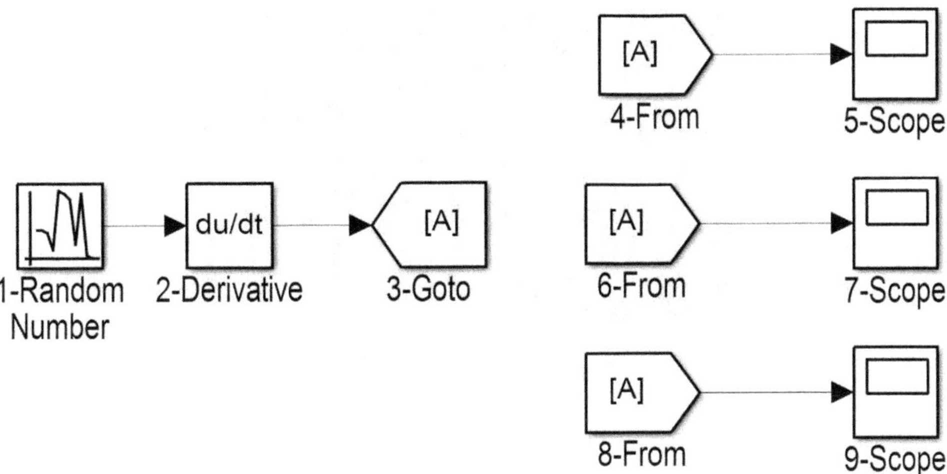

Figure 7.11 Simulink model for transferring data between input-output blocks without signals

Details of blocks are given in Table 7.3.

Table 7.3 Details of blocks - Transferring data between input-output blocks without signals

Name of block in model	Name of block in Simulink library	Source	Properties
1-Random number	Random number	Sources	---
2-Derivative	Derivative	Continuous	---
3-Goto	Goto	Signal routing	---
4-From	From	Signal routing	---
5-Scope	Scope	Sinks	---
6-From	From	Signal routing	---
7-Scope	Scope	Sinks	---
8-From	From	Signal routing	---
9-Scope	Scope	Sinks	---

Running the model with simulation time of 10 seconds, double clicking 5-scope block/ 7-scope block/9-scope block and then selecting auto scale option, plot shown in Figure 7.12 will be displayed.

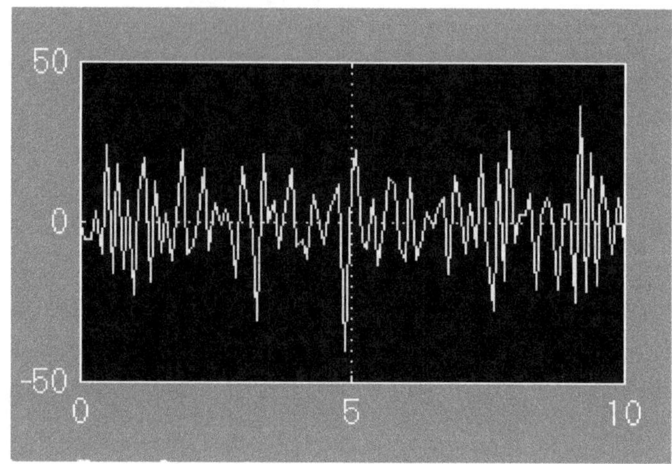

Figure 7.12 First derivative plot of random signal

7.2 INTEGRATION

Integration part of calculus is normally used for computing area under a response plot to obtain a significant physical quantity like root mean square (rms) value of dynamic acceleration. In simple physics sense integration of fluid flow yields to volume. Performing integration also tedious as is the case with differentiation. Equally Simulink offers a user friendly solution for performing integration. Examples given below brings out the capabilities of Simulink with respect to integration.

EXAMPLE 7.4

To build a Simulink model for generating digital data corresponding to variable frequency cosine wave, writing the same to mat file and matlab workspace and plotting with following parameters for the given variable frequency sine wave:

Initial frequency: 0.1 Hz; Total time: 100 sec; Frequency at the end of time: 1 Hz

The following blocks are used to build the model.

Chirp signal block is used to generate variable frequency sine wave, To file block is used to write the digital data to mat file and to workspace block is used to write the data to matlab workspace. In addition clock block is used to provide time stamping.

Associated Simulink model is shown in Figure 7.13.

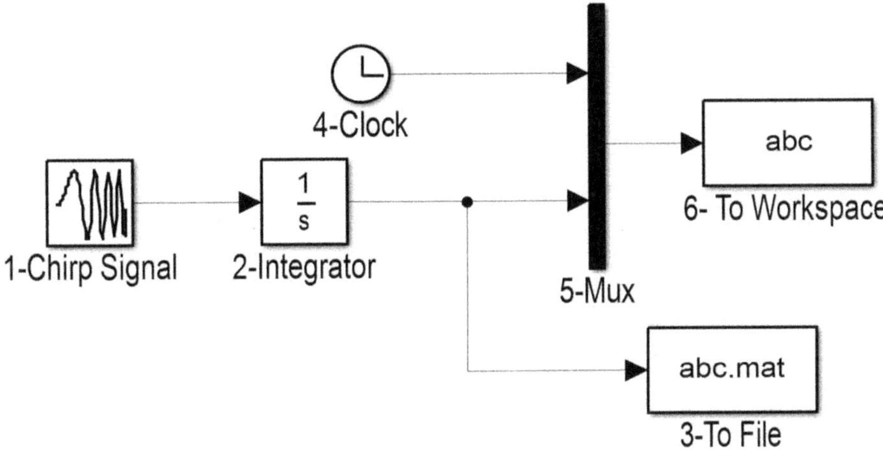

Figure 7.13 Simulink model for writing data to mat file & work space

Details of blocks are given in Table 7.4.

Table 7.4 Details of blocks - Writing data to mat file & work space

Name of block in model	Name of block in Simulink library	Source	Properties
1-Chirp signal	Chirp signal	Sources	---
2-Integrator	Integrator	Commonly used blocks	----
3-To file	To file	Sinks	File name: abc.mat
4-Clock	Clock	Sources	---
5-Mux	Mux	Commonly used blocks	Right mouse button – format - Show block name
6-To workspace	To workspace	Sinks	Variable name: abc.mat

Running the model with simulation time of 10 seconds, get into the matlab command window then type following (Outcome of to file block)

>>open abc

Then the window shown in Figure 7.14 will appear.

	1	2	3	4	5	6	7	8	9
1	0	0							
2	0.2000	0.0126							
3	0.4000	0.0506							
4	0.6000	0.1137							
5	0.8000	0.2013							
6	1	0.3123							
7	1.2000	0.4448							
8	1.4000	0.5969							
9	1.6000	0.7657							
10	1.8000	0.9481							
11	2.0000	1.1404							
12	2.2000	1.3386							
13	2.4000	1.5384							
14	2.6000	1.7351							
15	2.8000	1.9240							
16	3.0000	2.1003							
17	3.2000	2.2595							
18	3.4000	2.3972							

Figure 7.14 Matalb workspace showing the variable

Further typing the following in matlab command window generates a plot shown in Figure 7.15 (Outcome of to workspace block).

```
>> plot(abc(:,1),abc(:,2)); grid on
```

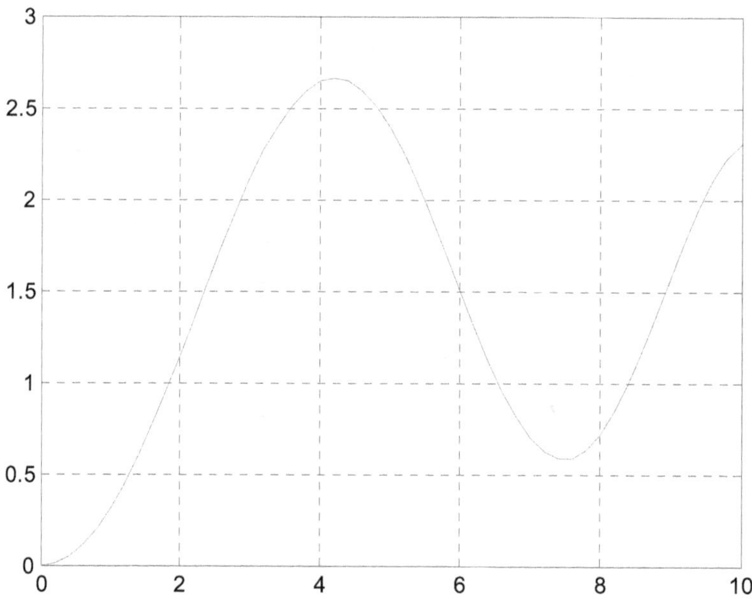

Figure 7.15 Plot of digital data corresponding to variable frequency cosine wave

EXAMPLE 7.5

To build a Simulink model for performing integration of sawtooth wave and plot the same as function of given sawtooth wave and to terminate simulation when the integrated value reaches 1.5654:

Following are the parameters of sawtooth wave:

Amplitude: 1; Frequency: 1 rad/sec;

The following blocks are used to build the model.

Signal generator block is used to generate sawtooth wave, XY graph block is used for plotting, relational operator block is used for imposing the given condition and stop simulation block is used to terminate the simulation when desired value is reached.

Associated Simulink model is shown in Figure 7.16.

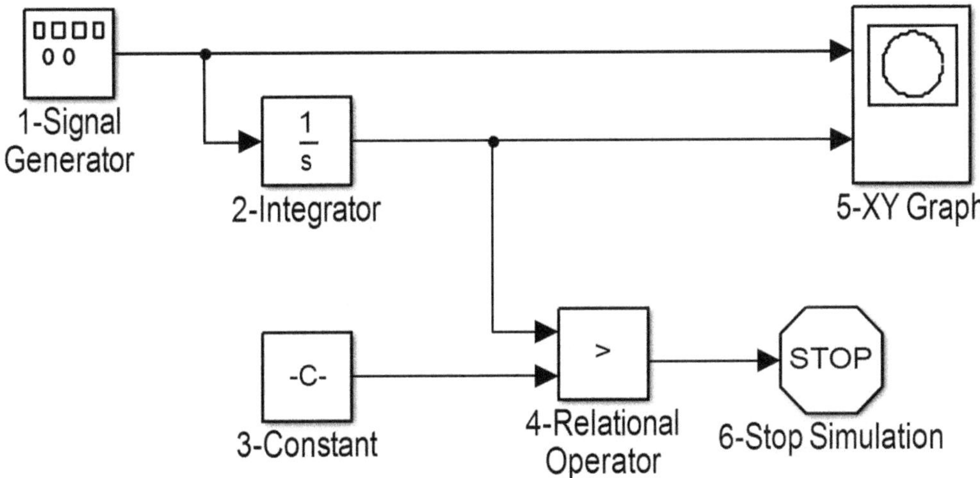

Figure 7.16 Simulink model for plotting integrated sawtooth wave

Details of blocks are given in Table 7.5.

Table 7.5 Details of blocks - Plotting integrated sawtooth wave

Name of block in model	Name of block in Simulink library	Source	Properties
1-Signal generator	Signal generator	Sources	---
2-Integrator	Integrator	Commonly used blocks	----
3-Constant	Constant	Commonly used blocks	Constant value: 1.5654
4-Relational operator	Relational operator	Commonly used blocks	Relational operator: >
5-XY graph	XY graph	Sinks	Y-max: 2
6-Stop simulation	Stop simulation	Sinks	---

Running the model with simulation time of 10 seconds, generates a plot shown in Figure 7.17.

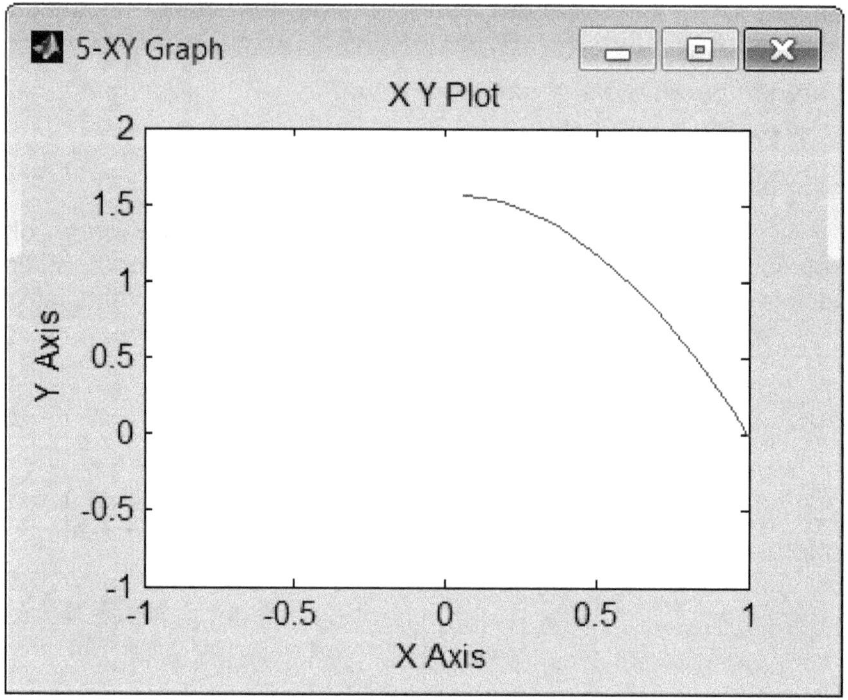

Figure 7.17 Plot of integrated sawtooth wave as a function of sawtooth wave

7.3 SUMMARY

Implementation of two basic operations of calculus viz. differentiation and integration in Simulink is brought out. Ease with which user can perform both in Simulink is highlighted. Functionality of slider gain block on contrary with conventional gain block is brought out. Significance of floating scope block compared to that of usual scope block is mentioned. Salient features of goto and from block are discussed. Further ways and means to write data to external sinks like workspace and file are also presented. Need for using Stop simulation block is elaborated.

CHAPTER 8

Plotting Signals

8.0 PLOTTING SIGNALS

Various signals are required to be analyzed to study the behavior of physical systems. For which graphical representation of signals will be more apt for effective interpretation and decision making. Hence signals are required to be plotted in time domain and if necessary in frequency domain. Apart from this certain operations like removing noise floor and adjusting DC shift also will be needed for which plotting of a given signal is essential. This chapter brings out various means adopted for plotting signals and also for associated other operations.

8.1 BASIC SIGNAL PLOTTING

Data of any type (Pressure, temperature, vibration, etc.) in general will be measured by sensor and same will be communicated to data acquisition system in form of digital data which needs to be plotted. Following example illustrates basic signal plotting capability of Simulink.

EXAMPLE 8.1

To build a Simulink model for plotting a signal from the following data.

X	0	2	2	4	4	6	6	8
Y	0	0	1	1	-1	-1	0	0

Signal builder block is used to generate the desired plot and in addition to this **digital clock** block is used for time stamping.

Associated Simulink model is shown in Figure 8.1.

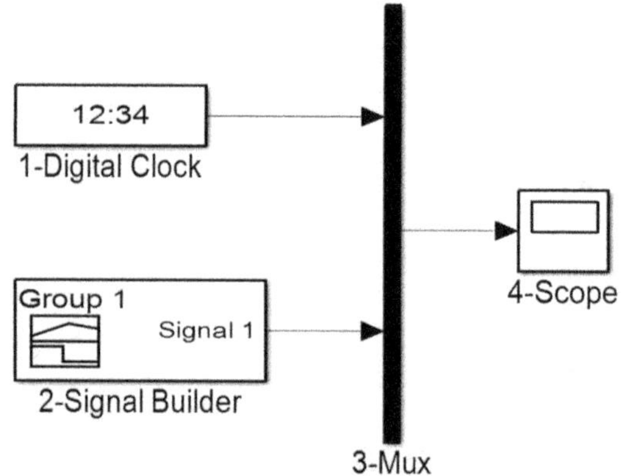

Figure 8.1 Simulink model for plotting the signal from the given data

Details of blocks are given in Table 8.1.

Table 8.1 Details of blocks- Plotting the signal from the given data

Name of block in model	Name of block in Simulink library	Source	Properties
1-Digital clock	Digital clock	Sources	Sample time: 4
2-Signal builder	Signal builder	Sources	Double clicking the block will generate a default plot and to create the desired plot, follow the procedure given below: If the data point (One with red diamond shape indicator) on the existing plot matches with respect to desired x or y value then position and click the left mouse button then a circle will be visible over diamond then enter the desired x value in T block and y value in Y block in the bottom side under 'Left point'. To create a new data point, select the particular line then press 'shift+left mouse buttons' and then select the data point and change its values. Make the following setting also: Double click the block and then select 'Axes' from top menu, further select 'Set T display limits' and type '8' in maximum block.
3-Mux	Mux	Commonly used blocks	Right mouse button – format - Show block name
4-Scope	Scope	Sinks	---

Running the model with simulation time of 8 seconds, double clicking **4-scope** block and then selecting auto scale option, plot shown in Figure 8.2 will be displayed.

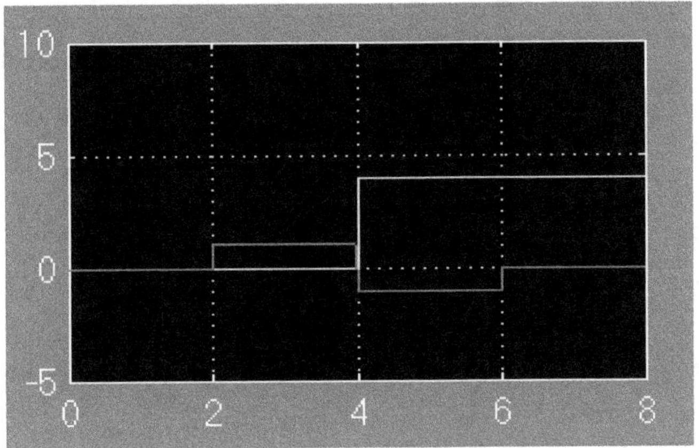

Figure 8.2 Plot of signal from data

8.2   PLOTTING SIGNAL WITH PRESET LIMITS

Often it will be needed to confine the signal after reaching a preset maximum limit. To demonstrate the same an example is presented below considering stepped signal with preset maximum limits.

EXAMPLE 8.2

To build a Simulink model for plotting a stepped signal which drops to zero after reaching a maximum value of 15 and repeat the same trend.

Counter free-running block is used to generate the desired plot and same is repeated with the aid of **counter limited** block also.

Associated Simulink model is shown in Figure 8.3.

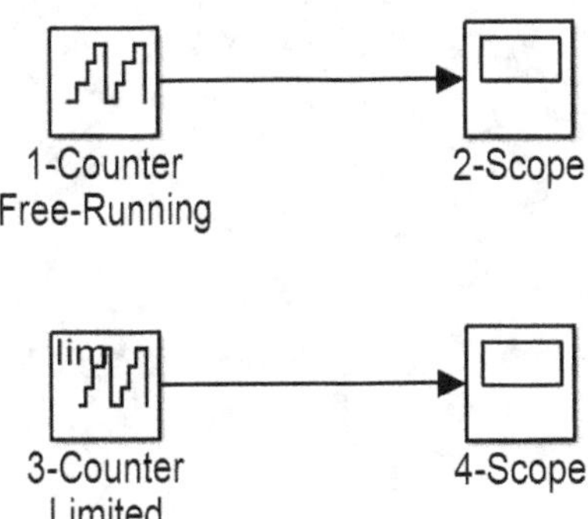

Figure 8.3 Simulink model for plotting the signal with limiting maximum value

Details of blocks are given in Table 8.2.

Table 8.2 Details of blocks - Plotting the signal with limiting maximum value

Name of block in model	Name of block in Simulink library	Source	Properties
1-Counter free-running	Counter free-running	Sources	Number of bits: 4
2-Scope	Scope	Sinks	---
3-Counter limited	Counter limited	Sources	Upper limit: 15
4-Scope	Scope	Sinks	---

Note: By stating number of bits as 4, **counter free-running** block considers the maximum limiting value as 2^4-1 = 15

Running the model with simulation time of 10 seconds, double clicking **2-scope** and **4-scope** blocks and then selecting auto scale option, plots shown in Figures 8.4 and 8.5 will be displayed respectively.

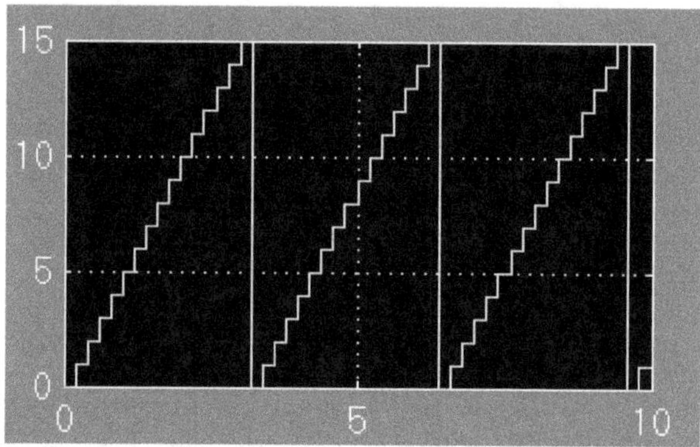

Figure 8.4 Plot with counter free-running block

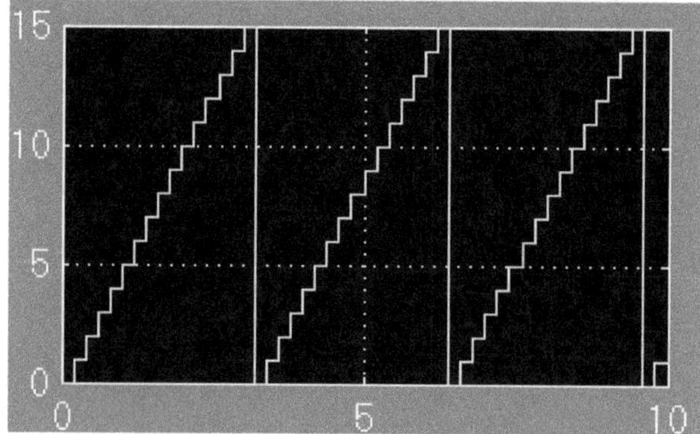

Figure 8.5 Plot with counter limited block

8.3   PLOTTING SIGNAL WITH SCALE FACTORS

In general magnitude of almost of all physical signals will be very less and viewing the same for further analysis will throw a challenge. Amplifying the signals with specified scale factor is a generally adopted solution for the said problem. Example below presents the implementation of same for a pulse signal.

EXAMPLE 8.3

To build a Simulink model for plotting a pulse signal without and with specified scale factors of 2, 3 and 4. Consider the following parameters for pulse signal:

Amplitude: 1; Period: 2 sec; Pulse width: 5

The following blocks are used to build the model.

Pulse generator block is used to generate pulse, **From workspace** block is used to feed scale factor values.

Associated Simulink model is shown in Figure 8.6.

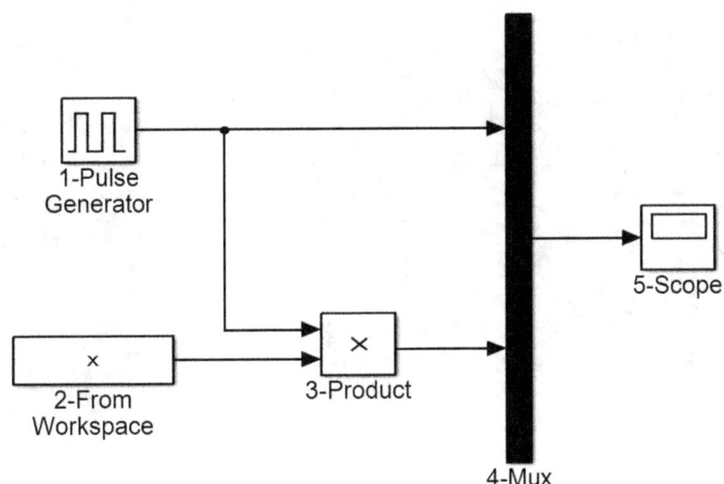

Figure 8.6 Simulink model for plotting a pulse signal without and with specified scale factors

Details of blocks are given in Table 8.3.

Table 8.3 Details of blocks - Plotting a pulse signal without and with specified scale factors

Name of block in model	Name of block in Simulink library	Source	Properties
1-Pulse generator	Pulse generator	Sources	Period: 2; Pulse width: 5
2-From workspace	From workspace	Sources	x

Table 8.3 Contd...

Name of block in model	Name of block in Simulink library	Source	Properties
3-Product	Product	Math operations	---
4-Mux	Mux	Commonly used blocks	Right mouse button – format - Show block name
5-Scope	Scope	Sinks	---

Get into the matlab command window then type following

>>x=[2 2 3 4];

Note: First element of vector 'x' i.e. 2 represents the time stamping, otherwise it doesn't play any role. Other elements represents the scale factors

Running the model with simulation time of 10 seconds, double clicking **5-scope** block and then selecting auto scale option, plot shown in Figure 8.7 will be displayed.

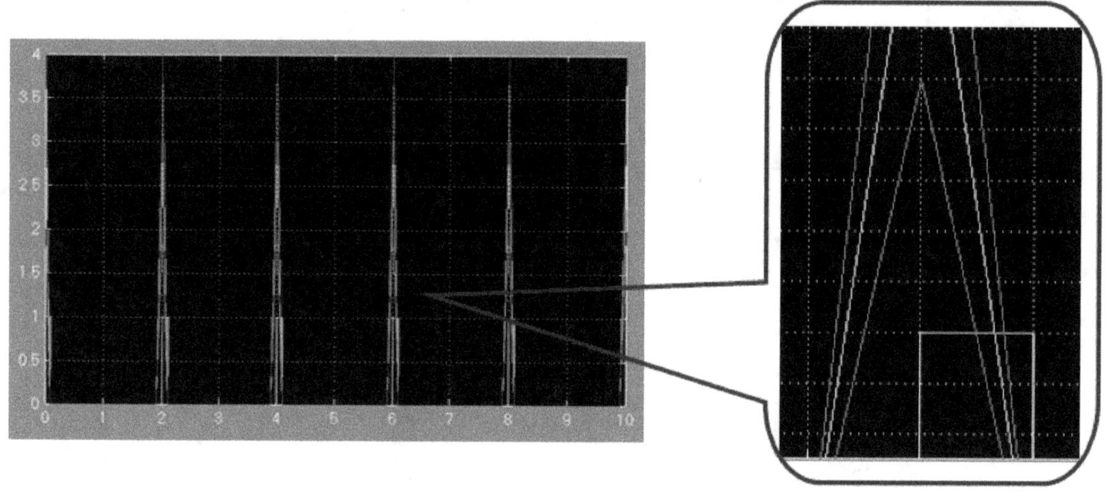

Figure 8.7 Plot of pulse signal

In the above plot yellow color represents pulse signal without scale factor, magenta color, cyan color and red color represents same signal with scale factors of 2, 3 and 4 respectively.

8.4 PLOTTING SIGNAL WITHIN A RANGE OF LIMITS

Setting lower and upper limits and accordingly confining the measured signal within that range will be needed in signal processing. Such instance is addressed using Simulink and the same is narrated through the example given below.

EXAMPLE 8.4

To build Simulink models for plotting random numbers without and with setting limits (Lower limit: -1 & upper limit: 1)

Simulink model is shown in Figure 8.8.

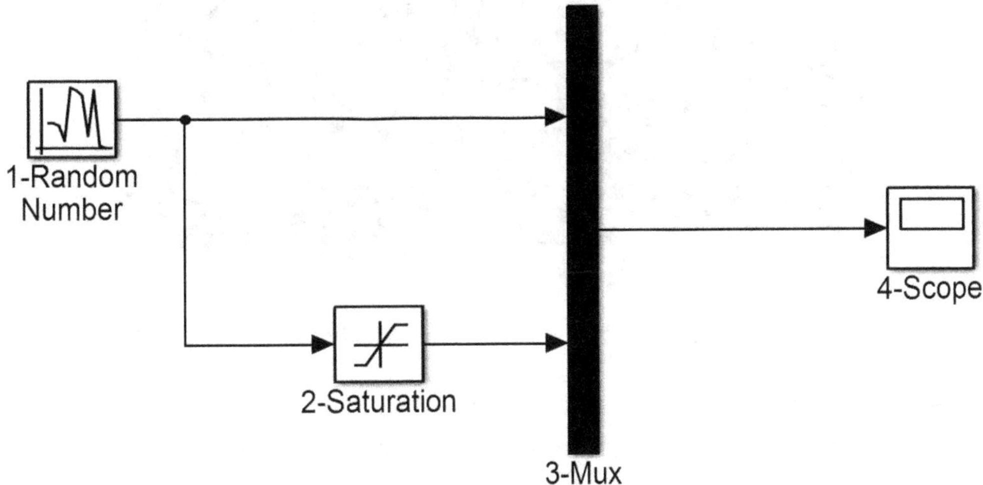

Figure 8.8 Simulink model for plotting random number series without and with limits

Details of blocks are given in Table 8.4.

Table 8.4 Details of blocks - Plotting random number series without and with limits

Name of block in model	Name of block in Simulink library	Source	Properties
1-Random number	Random number	Sources	---
2-Saturation	Saturation	Commonly used blocks	Upper limit: 1 Lower limit: -1
3-Mux	Mux	Commonly used blocks	Right mouse button – format - Show block name
4-Scope	Scope	Sinks	---

Upon running the model with simulation time of 10 seconds, double clicking **scope** block and then selecting auto scale option, plot shown in Figure 8.9 will be displayed.

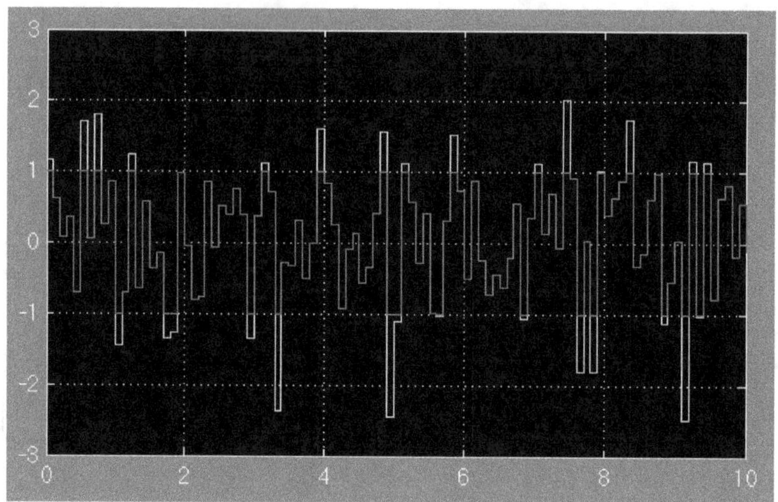

Figure 8.9 Plot of random number series without and with limits

In the above figure, yellow indicates plot of random number series as it is, wherein magenta indicates plot of same random number series with in limits of -1 to 1.

Note: If the result is below lower limit/beyond upper limit, it will be considered as the limiting value. For example if the lower limit is set to be -1 and the result is -2 it will be taken as -1.

8.5 PLOTTING SIGNAL WITH WEIGHTING FACTORS

Applying weighting factors (Both positive and negative) on the actual signal is a usual practice for statistical estimation of non-deterministic signals like random. Following example illustrates the same.

EXAMPLE 8.5

To build Simulink model for plotting random numbers with positive and negative weighting factor of 5:

This can be achieved by **Weighted sample time math** block.

Associated Simulink model is shown in Figure 8.10.

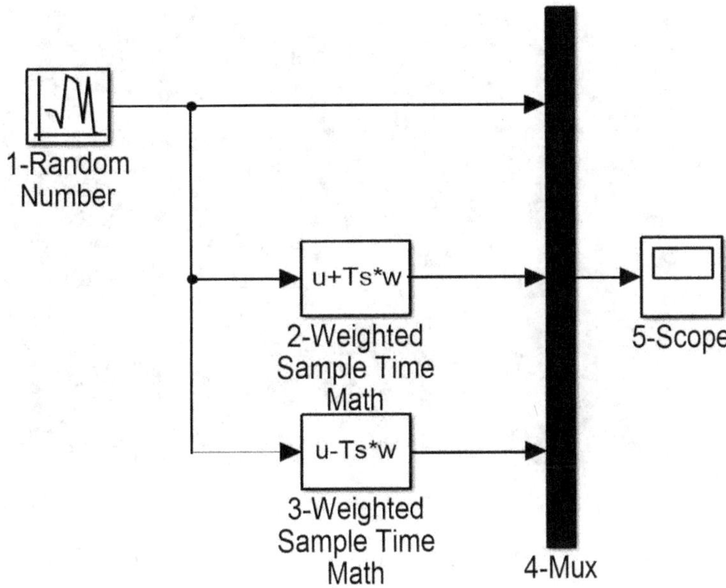

Figure 8.10 Simulink model for plotting random numbers with weighting factors

Details of blocks are given in Table 8.5.

Table 8.5 Details of blocks - Plotting random numbers with weighting factors

Name of block in model	Name of block in Simulink library	Source	Properties
1-Random number	Random number	Sources	---
2-Weighted sample time math	Weighted sample time math	Math operations	Operation: + Weight value: 5
3-Weighted sample time math	Weighted sample time math	Math operations	Operation: - Weight value: 5
4-Mux	Mux	Commonly used blocks	Number of inputs=3 Right mouse button – format - Show block name
5-Scope	Scope	Sinks	---

Running the model with simulation time of 10 seconds, double clicking **scope** block and then selecting auto scale option, plot shown in Figure 8.11 will be displayed.

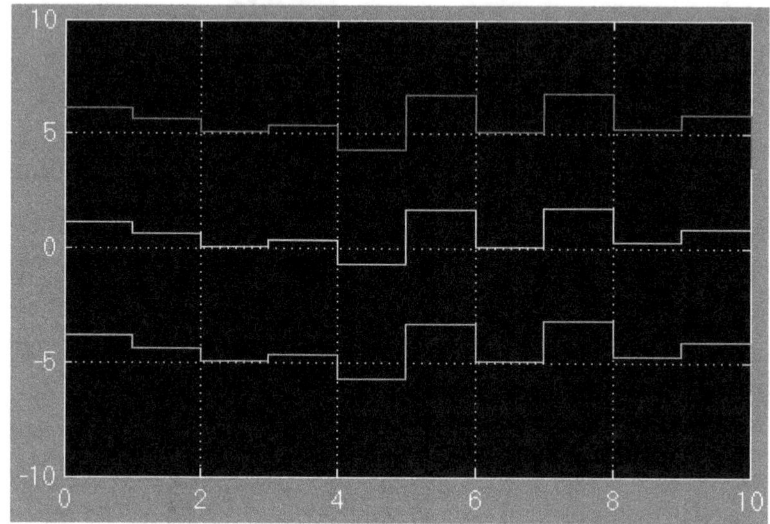

Figure 8.11 Plot of random numbers with weighting factors

In the above plot yellow color represents the input random signal, magenta color represents input random signal with positive weighting factor and cyan color represents input random signal with negative weighting factor respectively.

Note: Weighted sample time math block also supports multiplication, division, etc.

8.6 PLOTTING SIGNAL WITH ELIMINATING NOISE FLOOR

In the practical scenario actual signal will be contaminated with noise component like electrical noise and its associated harmonics. Removing such noise floor is essentially required so as to avoid misinterpretation of the actual signal. An example for same is given below.

EXAMPLE 8.6

To build a Simulink model for plotting a random signal after removing noise floor with a magnitude of -0.5 to 0.5.

Dead zone block and **dead zone dynamic** blocks are used to simulate the upper and lower bands for noise floor. With these blocks any signal component with in the band set i.e. -0.5 to 0.5 becomes zero and rest all will be attenuated by 0.5 on both positive and negative side. Functioning of **dead zone dynamic** block is identical to that of **dead zone** block except defining band limits externally. Though the functionality is same both are used just for the sake of demonstration.

Simulink model is shown in Figure 8.12.

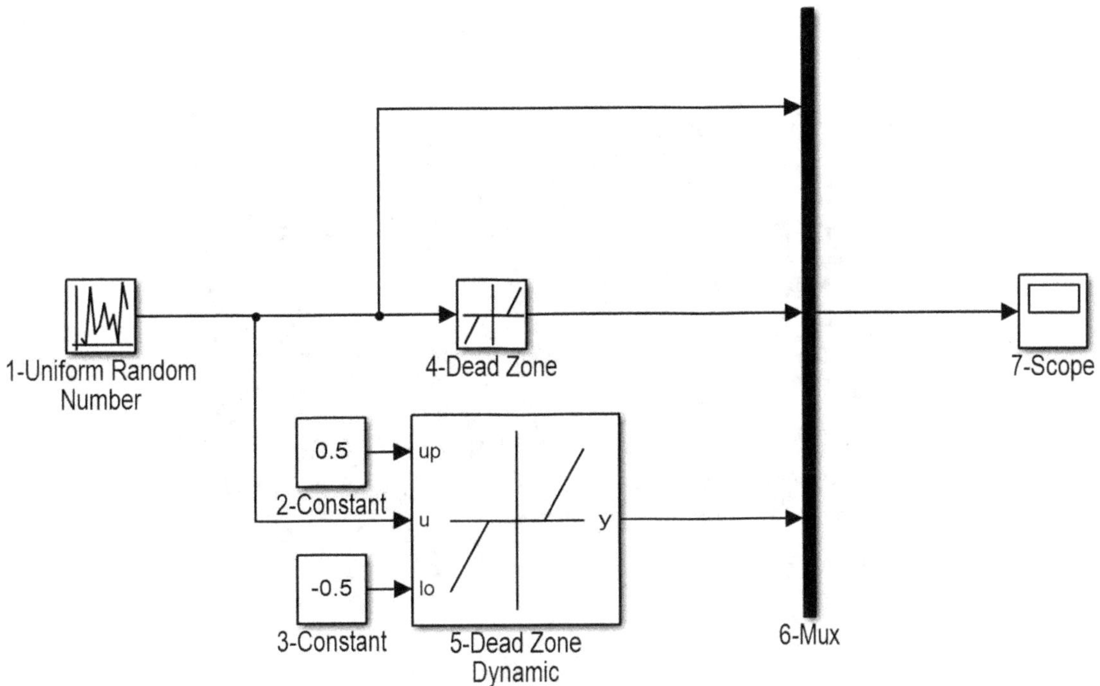

Figure 8.12 Simulink model for plotting a random signal after removing noise floor

Details of blocks are given in Table 8.6.

Table 8.6 Details of blocks- Plotting a random signal after removing noise floor

Name of block in model	Name of block in Simulink library	Source	Properties
1-Unifrom random number	Uniform random number	Sources	---
2-Constant	Constant	Commonly used blocks	Constant value: 0.5
3-Constant	Constant	Commonly used blocks	Constant value: -0.5
4-Dead zone	Dead zone	Discontinuities	Start of dead zone: -0.5 End of dead zone: 0.5
5-Dead zone dynamic	Dead zone dynamic	Discontinuities	---
6-Mux	Mux	Commonly used blocks	Right mouse button – format - Show block name Number of inputs:3
7-Scope	Scope	Sinks	----

Running the model with simulation time of 10 seconds, double clicking **scope** block and then selecting auto scale option, plot shown in Figure 8.13 will be displayed.

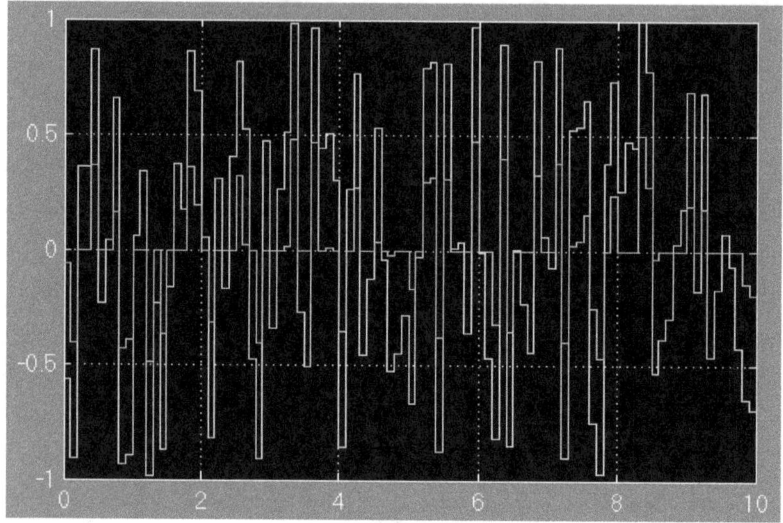

Figure 8.13 Plot of random signal before & after removing noise floor

In the above plot yellow color represents the random signal with noise floor and magenta and cyan represents random signal after removing noise floor with **dead zone** and **dead zone dynamic** blocks respectively. However as the functionality of both the blocks is identical magenta and cyan color gets merged.

8.7 PLOTTING SIGNAL WITH PHASE ADJUSTMENT

Phase adjustment will be done between two signals for the sake of correlation. Two such signals (Sine and cosine) are considered for adjustment of phase before plotting with the aid of Simulink and the associated example is given below.

EXAMPLE 8.7

Parameters for sine wave are as follows:

Amplitude: 1; Frequency: 1 rad/sec; Phase: 0, Sample time: 0.01 seconds.

We know that the phase difference between sine and cosine waves is 90^0 i.e. $\Pi/2$. Same is modeled using three different delay blocks that are **transport delay, variable time delay** and **variable transport delay** blocks.

Simulink model is shown in Figure 8.14.

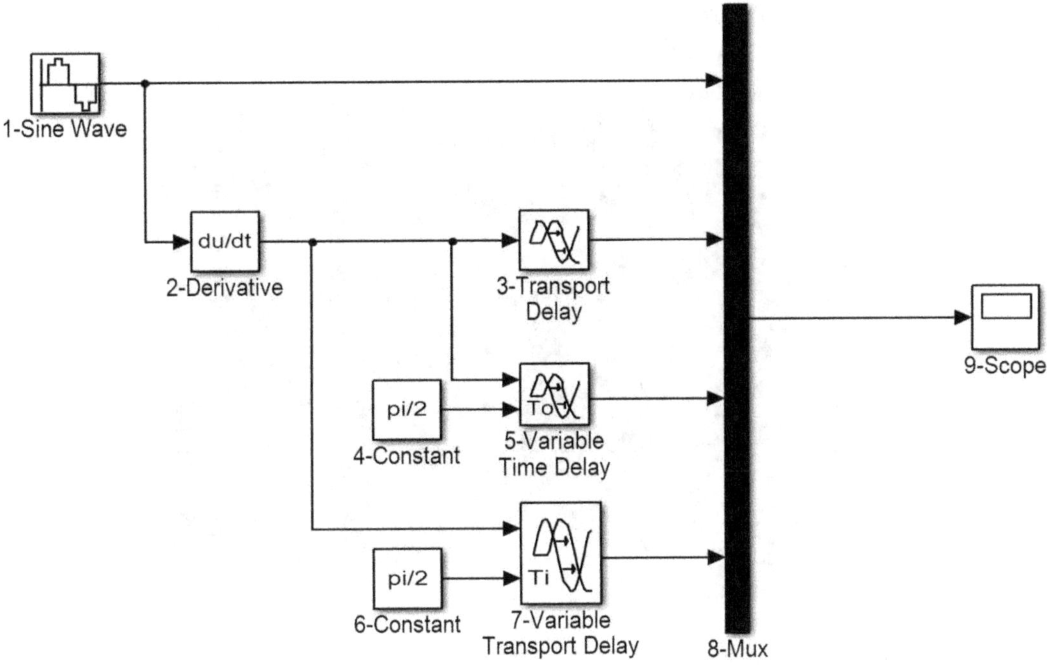

Figure 8.14 Simulink model for plotting sine and cosine waves with phase adjustment

Details of blocks are given in Table 8.7.

Table 8.7 Details of blocks - Plotting sine and cosine waves with phase adjustment

Name of block in model	Name of block in Simulink library	Source	Properties
1-Sine wave	Sine wave	Sources	Frequency: 1 Sample time: 0.01
2-Derivative	Derivative	Continuous	---
3-Transport delay	Transport delay	Continuous	Time delay: pi/2
4-Constant	Constant	Commonly used blocks	Constant value = pi/2
5-Variable time delay	Variable time delay	Continuous	---
6-Constant	Constant	Commonly used blocks	Constant value = pi/2
7-Variable transport delay	Variable transport delay	Continuous	---
8-Mux	Mux	Commonly used blocks	Right mouse button – format - Show block name; Number of inputs: 4
9-Scope	Scope	Sinks	----

Running the model with simulation time of 20 seconds, double clicking **scope** block and then selecting auto scale option, plot shown in Figure 8.15 will be displayed.

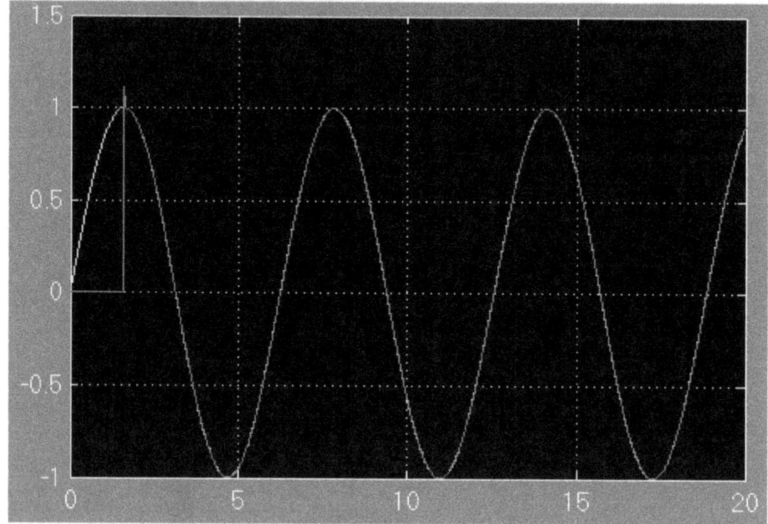

Figure 8.15 Plot of sine and cosine waves with phase adjustment

Yellow color represents sine wave and magenta, cyan and red (All 3 Merged) indicates cosine wave with phase difference of 90^0 using **transport delay, variable time delay** and **variable transport delay** blocks respectively.

It is evident that cosine wave is merged with sine wave after the set time delay.

Note: Transport delay block needs delay to be specified within function block parameters

Whereas **variable time delay** and **variable transport delay** blocks call for external definition of delay through second signal port.

However **variable transport delay** block can be used for simulating variable transport delay process like flow of fluids in a conduit.

8.8 PLOTTING SIGNALS WITH ADJUSTING MEAN SHIFT

Mean shift is a problem that will normally be encountered in signal measurement due to certain problems associated with measurement setup viz. base strain and temperature strain. Mean shift needs to be adjusted to zero before processing the signal otherwise amplitude of the signal will be misinterpreted. Example below simulates such phenomenon in Simulink.

EXAMPLE 8.8

To build Simulink model for plotting sine wave, sum of sine and cosine waves without and with mean shift with following parameters:

Amplitude = 2, Frequency = 1 rad/sec, Mean shift = 5

This can be achieved by **bias** block.

Associated Simulink model is shown in Figure 8.16.

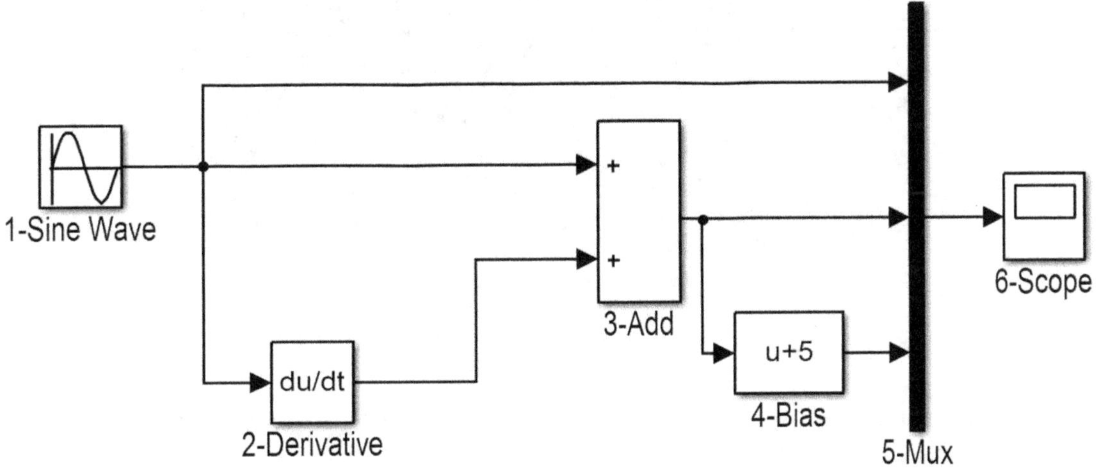

Figure 8.16 Simulink model for plotting sine and cosine signals with out and with mean shift

Details of blocks are given in Table 8.8.

Table 8.8 Details of blocks - Plotting sine and cosine signals with out and with mean shift

Name of block in model	Name of block in Simulink library	Source	Properties
1-Sine wave	Sine wave	Commonly used blocks	Amplitude:2 Frequency: 1
2-Derivative	Derivative	Continuous	---
3-Add	Add	Math operations	---
4-Bias	Bias	Math operations	Bias: 5
5-Mux	Mux	Commonly used blocks	Number of inputs=3 Right mouse button – format - Show block name
6-Scope	Scope	Sinks	---

Running the model with simulation time of 10 seconds, double clicking **scope** block and then selecting auto scale option, plot shown in Figure 8.17 will be displayed.

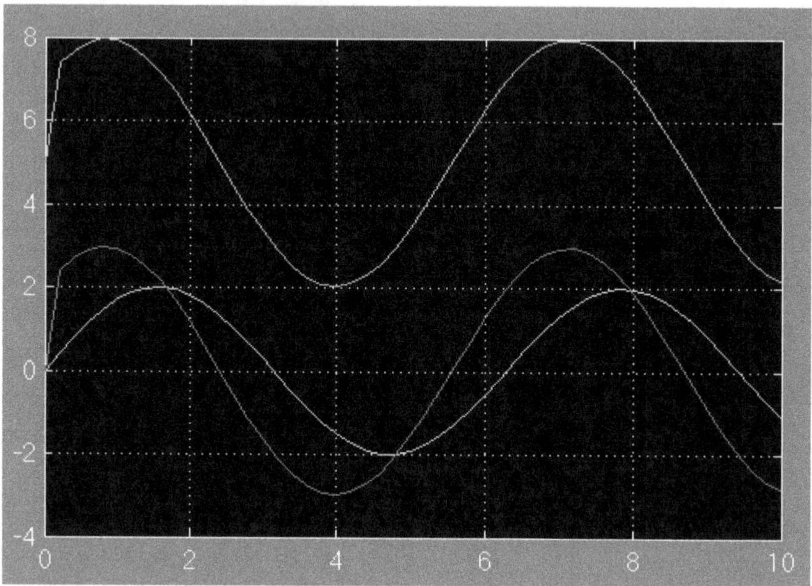

Figure 8.17 Plot of sine and cosine signals with out and with mean shift

In the above plot yellow color represents the sine signal, magenta color and cyan color represents sum of sine and cosine waves without mean shift and with mean shift respectively.

8.9 CLIPPING THE SIGNAL BEFOR PLOTTING

Attenuating the measured signal with specified saturation values is a rare requirement. This phenomenon is simulated in Simulink through the example given below.

EXAMPLE 8.9

To build a Simulink model for plotting a cosine signal after clipping with limits of -1 to 1.

Consider the following for sine wave:

Amplitude = 1; Frequency = 0.25 Hz (Pi/2 rad)

Saturation block and **saturation dynamic** blocks are used to simulate the clipping with upper and lower bands. With these blocks input signal will be confined to limits set both positive and negative side. Functioning of **saturation dynamic** block is identical to that of **saturation** block except defining clipping limits externally. Though the functionality is same, both the blocks are used just for the sake of demonstration.

Simulink model is shown in Figure 8.18.

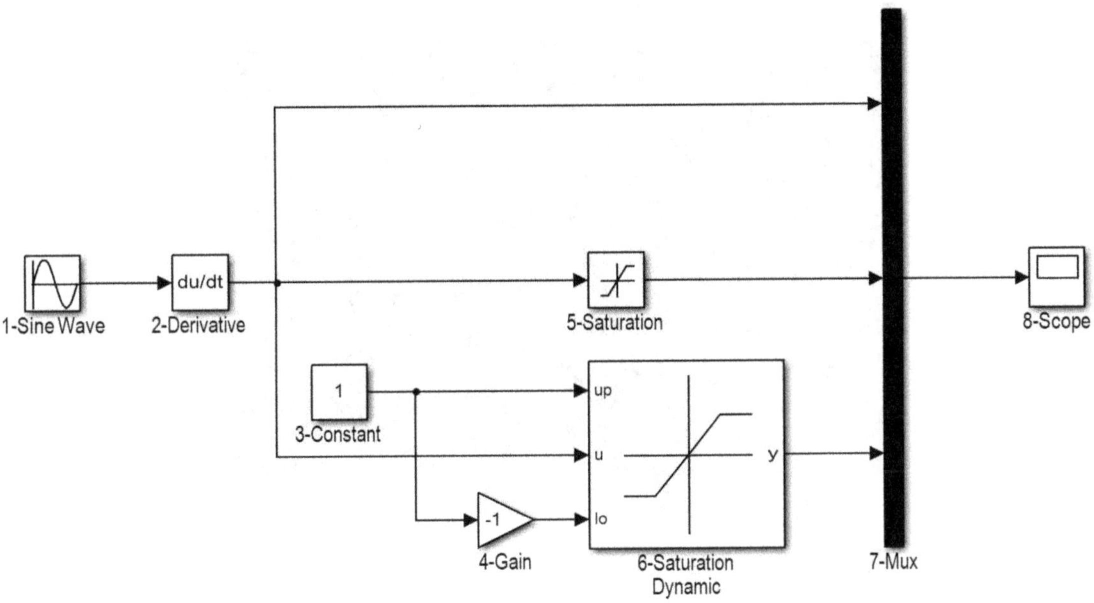

Figure 8.18 Simulink model for plotting cosine signal with clipping

Details of blocks are given in Table 8.9.

Table 8.9 Details of blocks - Plotting cosine signal with clipping

Name of block in model	Name of block in Simulink library	Source	Properties
1-Sine wave	Sine wave	Sources	Amplitude: 1 Frequency: pi/2
2-Derivative	Derivative	Continuous	----
3-Constant	Constant	Commonly used blocks	Constant value: 1
4-Gain	Gain	Commonly used blocks	Property-Gain: -1
5-Saturation	Saturation	Discontinuities	Upper limit: 1 Lower limit: -1
6-Saturation dynamic	Saturation dynamic	Discontinuities	----
7-Mux	Mux	Commonly used blocks	Right mouse button-Format-Show block name Number of inputs: 3
8-Scope	Scope	Sinks	-----

Running the model with simulation time of 10 seconds, double clicking **scope** block and then selecting auto scale option, plot shown in Figure 8.19 will be displayed.

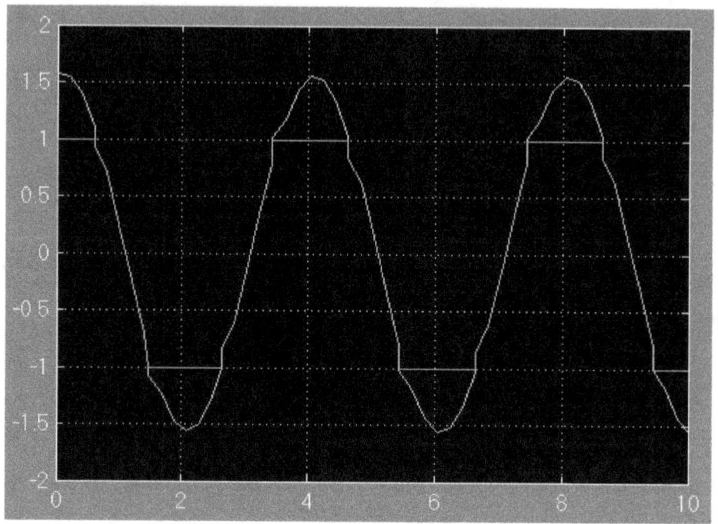

Figure 8.19 Plot of cosine signal without and with clipping

In the above plot yellow color represents the cosine signal and magenta and cyan represents cosine signal after clipping with **saturation** and **saturation dynamic** blocks respectively. However as the functionality of both the blocks is identical magenta and cyan color gets merged.

8.10 INDICATION OF SIGNAL CROSSOVER

Marking the time instances as and when signal crosses specified lower and upper bounds will be helpful for the user to make certain judgment. The following example brings out way to build the Simulink model for such requirement.

EXAMPLE 8.10

To build Simulink model for

   (i)   Plotting sine wave with following parameters:
        Amplitude = 2, Frequency = 0.25 Hz = pi/2 rad/sec
  (ii)   Setting lower bound of -1.5 and then indicate graphically wherever the input signal go below the lower bound
 (iii)   Setting upper bound of 1.5 and then indicate graphically wherever the input signal go beyond the upper bound

The following blocks are used to build the model.

  (i) **Sine wave** block and **scope** block are used
 (ii) **Check static lower bound** block is used with following function block parameters.

Lower bound: -1.5, Uncheck **stop simulation when assertion fails** option, check **output assertion signal** option and select **graphic** in **select icon type** option.

For accomplishing the same

Check dynamic lower bound block is also used with following function block parameters.

Uncheck **stop simulation when assertion fails** option, check **output assertion signal** option and select **graphic** in **select icon type** option.

Note: Functioning of **Check dynamic lower bound** block is same as that of **Check static lower bound** block except the difference of defining lower bound externally through a constant.

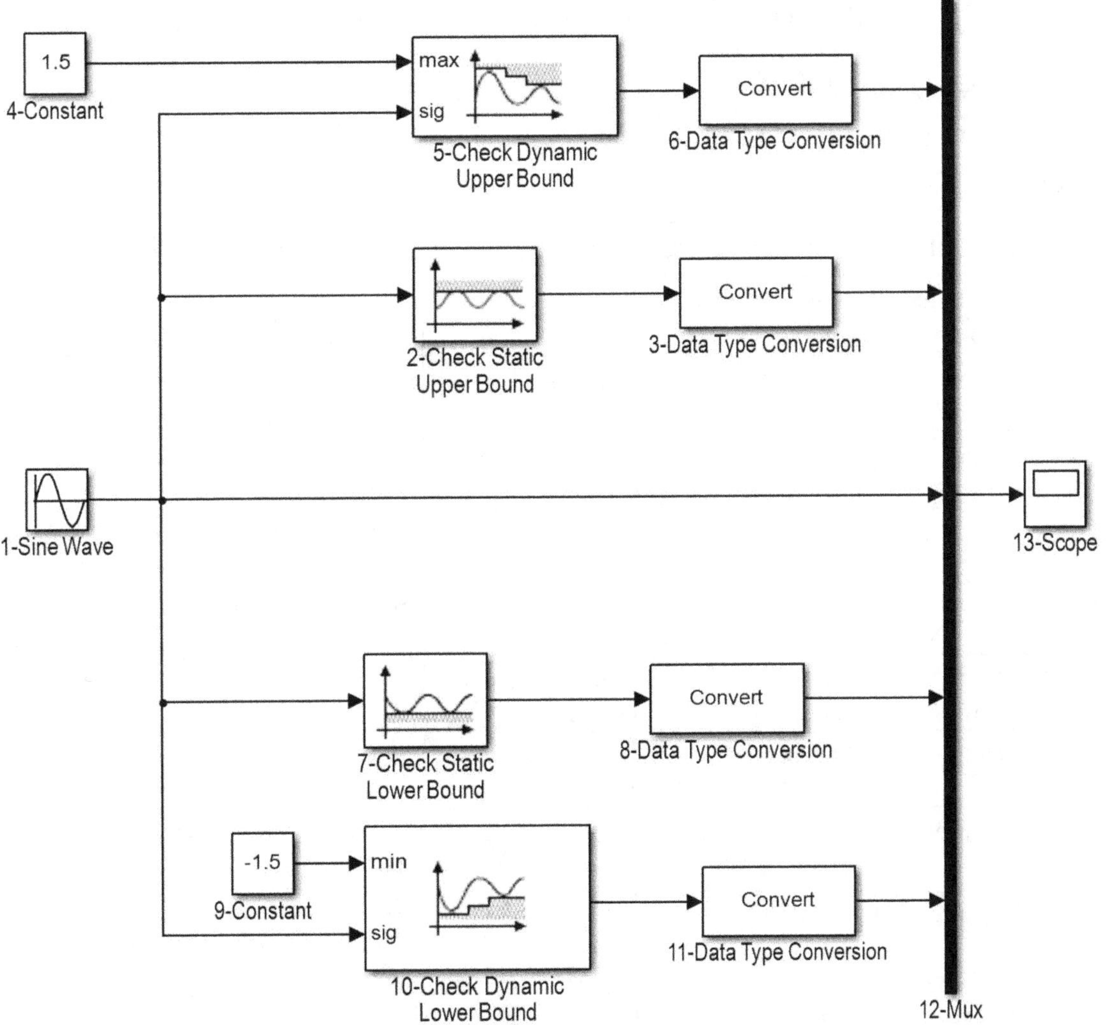

Figure 8.20 Simulink model for plotting sine signal with static lower and upper bounds

(i) **Check static upper bound** block is used with following function block parameters.

Upper bound: 1.5, Uncheck **stop simulation when assertion fails** option, check **output assertion signal** option and select **graphic** in **select icon type** option.

For accomplishing the same

Check dynamic upper bound block is also used with following function block parameters.

Uncheck **stop simulation when assertion fails** option, check **output assertion signal** option and select **graphic** in **select icon type** option.

Note: Functioning of **Check dynamic upper bound** block is same as that of **Check static upper bound** block except the difference of defining upper bound externally through a constant.

Data type conversion block is used to convert Boolean to double everywhere.

Associated Simulink model is shown in Figure 8.20.

Details of blocks are given in Table 8.10.

Table 8.10 Details of blocks - Plotting sine signal with static lower and upper bounds

Name of block in model	Name of block in Simulink library	Source	Properties
1-Sine wave	Sine wave	Sources	Amplitude:2 Frequency: pi/2 rad/sec
2-Check static upper bound	Check static upper bound	Model verification	Upper bound: 1.5 Uncheck 'stop simulation when assertion fails' Check 'output assertion signal' Select 'graphic' from 'select icon type' option
3-Data type conversion	Data type conversion	Commonly used blocks	---
4-Constant	Constant	Commonly used blocks	Constant value: 1.5
5-Check dynamic upper bound	Check dynamic upper bound	Model verification	Uncheck 'stop simulation when assertion fails' Check 'output assertion signal' Select 'graphic' from 'select icon type' option
6-Data type conversion	Data type conversion	Commonly used blocks	---

Table 8.10 *Contd...*

Name of block in model	Name of block in Simulink library	Source	Properties
7-Check static lower bound	Check static lower bound	Model verification	Lower bound: -1.5 Uncheck 'stop simulation when assertion fails' Check 'output assertion signal' Select 'graphic' from 'select icon type' option
8-Data type conversion	Data type conversion	Commonly used blocks	---
9-Constant	Constant	Commonly used blocks	Constant value: -1.5
10-Check dynamic lower bound	Check dynamic lower bound	Model verification	Uncheck 'stop simulation when assertion fails' Check 'output assertion signal' Select 'graphic' from 'select icon type' option
11-Data type conversion	Data type conversion	Commonly used blocks	---
12-Mux	Mux	Commonly used blocks	Number of inputs: 5 Right mouse button – format - Show block name
13-Scope	Scope	Sinks	---

Running the model with simulation time of 10 seconds, double clicking **scope** block and then selecting auto scale option, plot shown in Figure 8.21 will be displayed.

In the above plot

Cyan color represents input sine signal

Magenta color represents graphical indication of upper bound generated by **check static upper bound** block overlapped on input sine signal. From this it is clearly evident that magenta plot comes down to '0' whenever input sine signal is crossing the set upper band i.e. 1.5, otherwise it remains at 1. Yellow color represents the same generated by **check dynamic upper bound** block and the same is not visible as it is merged with magenta color plot.

Green color represents graphical indication of lower bound generated by **check dynamic lower bound** block overlapped on input sine signal. From this it is clearly evident that green plot comes down to '0' whenever input sine signal is crossing the set lower band i.e. -1.5, otherwise it remains at 1. Red color represents the same generated by **check static lower bound** block and the same is not visible as it is merged with green color plot.

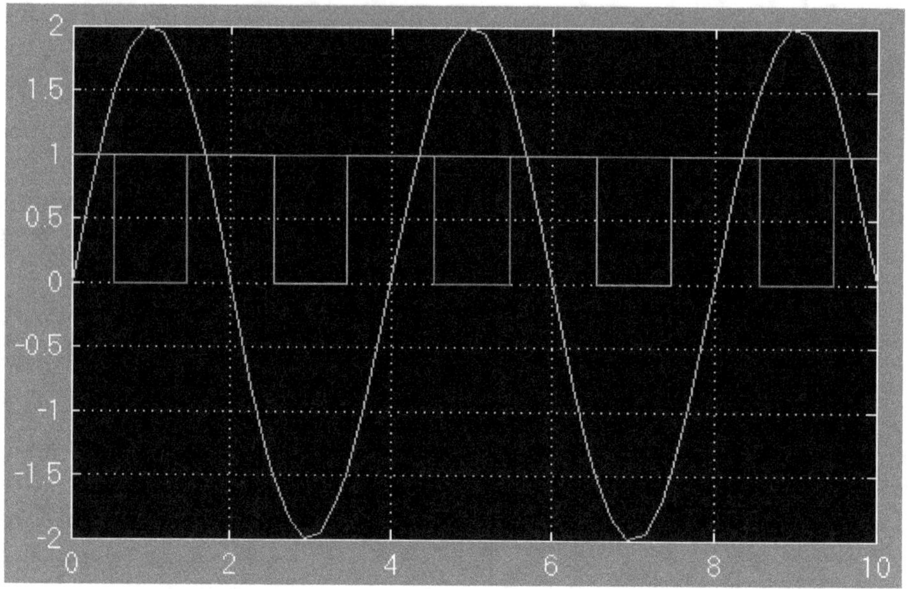

Figure 8.21 Plot of sine signal with static lower and upper bounds

8.11 INDICATION OF SIGNAL TREND

Indication of signal trend remaining/going beyond the range set is another requirement in signal processing. Example given below shows how to model the same in Simulink.

EXAMPLE 8.11

To build Simulink model for

(i) Plotting sine wave with following parameters:
Amplitude = 2, Frequency = 0.25 Hz = pi/2 rad/sec

(ii) Setting the range of -1 to 1 and then indicate graphically wherever the input signal exceeds the range

The following blocks are used to build the model.

(i) **Sine wave** block and **scope** block are used

(ii) Same is addressed in two ways.

Check static gap block is used with following function block parameters.

Upper bound: 1; Lower bound: -1, Uncheck **stop simulation when assertion fails** option, check **output assertion signal** option and select **graphic** in **select icon type** option. With this block resulting plot yields to '0' for the duration when input signal lying in the stated range, otherwise remains at '1'

Alternatively

Check dynamic gap block is used with following function block parameters.

Uncheck **stop simulation when assertion fails** option, check **output assertion signal** option and select **graphic** in **select icon type** option. With this block also resulting plot yields to '0' for the duration when input signal lying in the stated range, otherwise remains at '1'

Note: Functioning of **Check dynamic gap** block is same as that of **Check static gap** block except the difference of defining upper bound and lower bound externally through constants.

Check static range block is used with following function block parameters.

Upper bound: 1; Lower bound: -1, Uncheck **stop simulation when assertion fails** option, check **output assertion signal** option and select **graphic** in **select icon type** option. With this block resulting plot yields to '0' for the duration when input signal goes out of stated range, otherwise remains at '1'

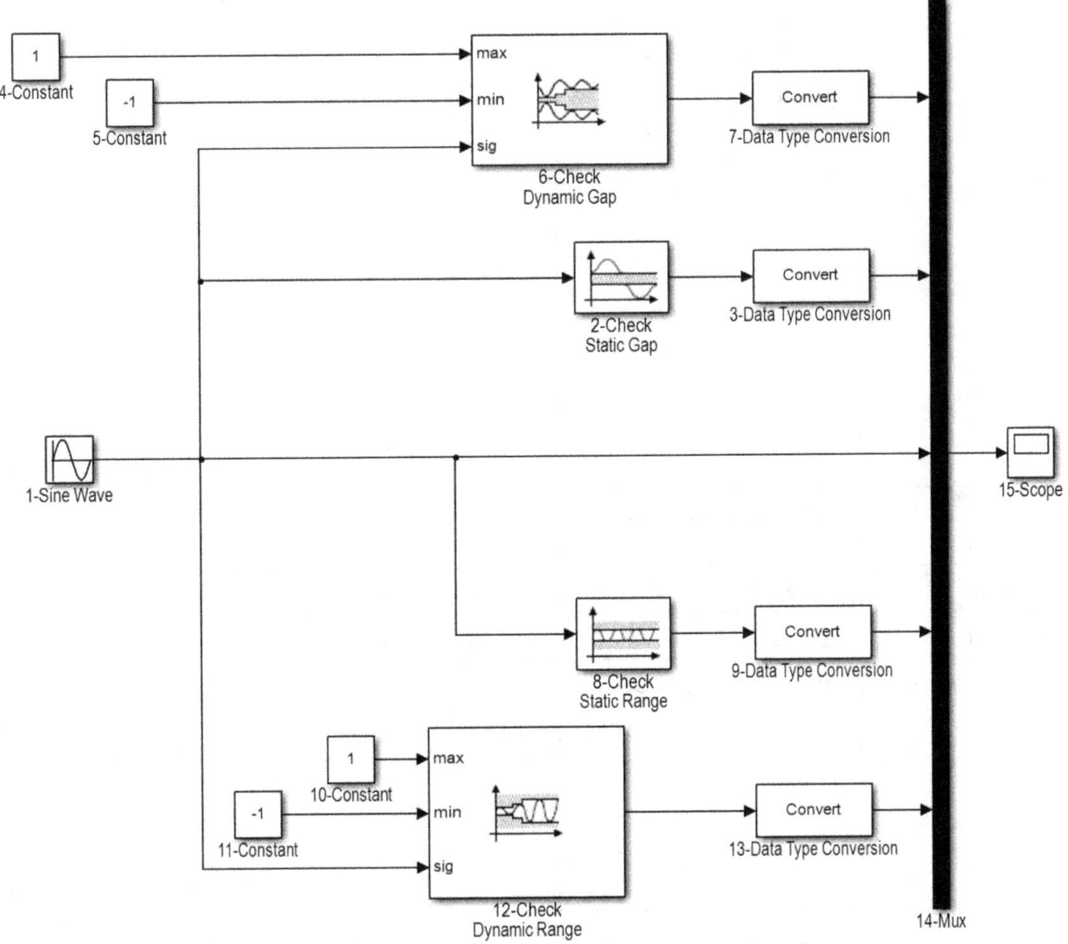

Figure 8.22 Simulink model for plotting sine signal with range setting

Alternatively

Check dynamic range block is used with following function block parameters.

Uncheck **stop simulation when assertion fails** option, check **output assertion signal** option and select **graphic** in **select icon type** option. With this block also resulting plot yields to '0' for the duration when input signal lying in the stated range, otherwise remains at '1'

Note: Functioning of **Check dynamic range** block is same as that of **Check static range** block except the difference of defining upper bound and lower bound externally through constants.

Associated Simulink model is shown in Figure 8.22.

Details of blocks are given in Table 8.11.

Table 8.11 Details of blocks - Plotting sine signal with range setting

Name of block in model	Name of block in Simulink library	Source	Properties
1-Sine wave	Sine wave	Commonly used blocks	Amplitude:2 Frequency: pi/2
2-Check static gap	Check static gap	Model verification	Upper bound: 1 Lower bound: -1 Uncheck 'stop simulation when assertion fails' Check 'output assertion signal' Select 'graphic' from 'select icon type' option
3-Data type conversion	Data type conversion	Commonly used blocks	---
4-Constant	Constant	Commonly used blocks	Constant value: 1
5-Constant	Constant	Commonly used blocks	Constant value: -1
6-Check dynamic gap	Check dynamic gap	Model verification	Uncheck 'stop simulation when assertion fails' Check 'output assertion signal' Select 'graphic' from 'select icon type' option
7-Data type conversion	Data type conversion	Commonly used blocks	---

Table 8.11 Contd...

Name of block in model	Name of block in Simulink library	Source	Properties
8-Check static range	Check static range	Model verification	Upper bound: 1 Lower bound: -1 Uncheck 'stop simulation when assertion fails' Check 'output assertion signal' Select 'graphic' from 'select icon type' option
9-Data type conversion	Data type conversion	Commonly used blocks	---
10-Constant	Constant	Commonly used blocks	Constant value: 1
11-Constant	Constant	Commonly used blocks	Constant value: -1
12-Check dynamic range	Check dynamic range	Model verification	Uncheck 'stop simulation when assertion fails' Check 'output assertion signal' Select 'graphic' from 'select icon type' option
13-Data type conversion	Data type conversion	Commonly used blocks	---
14-Mux	Mux	Commonly used blocks	Number of inputs: 5 Right mouse button – format - Show block name
15-Scope	Scope	Sinks	---

Running the model with simulation time of 10 seconds, double clicking **scope** block and then selecting auto scale option, plot shown in Figure 8.23 will be displayed.

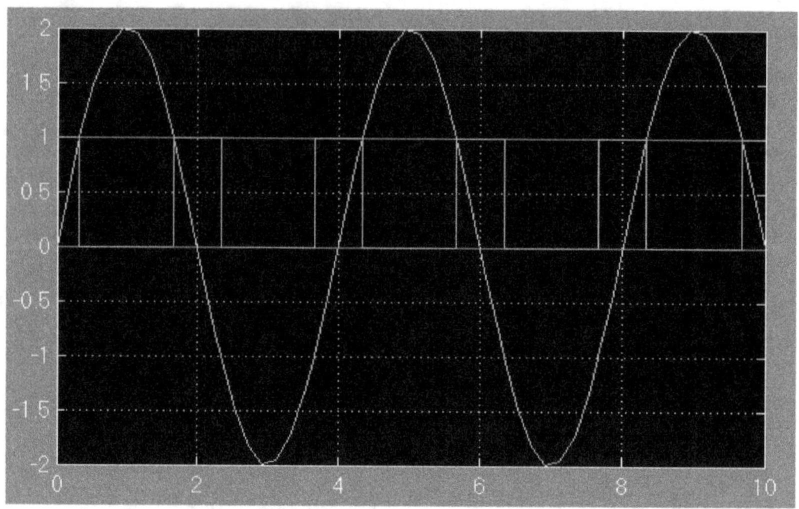

Figure 8.23 Plot of sine signal with range setting

In the above plot

Cyan color represents input sine signal

Magenta color represents graphical indication of **check static gap** block. From this plot it is evident that it yields to '0' for the duration when input signal lying in the stated range, otherwise remains at '1'. Yellow color represents the same generated by **check dynamic gap** block and the same is not visible as it is merged with magenta color plot.

Green color represents graphical indication of **check dynamic range** block. From this plot it is evident that it yields to '0' for the duration when input signal goes out of stated range, otherwise remains at '1'. Red color represents the same generated by **check static range** block and the same is not visible as it is merged with green color plot.

8.12 SUMMARY

Basic signal plotting capabilities of Simulink are illustrated with examples. Plotting signals with preset limits is demonstrated. Imposing scale factors over actual signal is considered. Requirement of plotting signal within range of limits is addressed. Application of weighting factors on actual signal for statistical estimations of certain signals is mentioned. Technic of eliminating noise floor using Simulink before plotting signal is put forwarded. An example narrating phase adjustment of signals for the sake of correlation is brought out. Addressing practical problem with mean shift associated with signals is given due consideration. Clipping the signal before plotting is elaborated through an example. Indication of signal crossover by setting lower and upper bounds and also range is explained.

CHAPTER 9

Solving Differential Equations

9.0 DIFFERENTIAL EQUATIONS

Differential equations in general represents the governing relationship corresponding to physical phenomenon and associated physical quantities. As the said governing equations consists of higher order derivatives it needs to solve them to obtain the actual physical quantities. Solving higher order differential equations is cumbersome for which Simulink offers promising solution. Another unique merit with Simulink is that it extracts the behavior of physical quantity directly from differential equation. This chapter brings out the methodology that needs to be followed for solving differential equations in Simulink.

9.1 SOLVING DIFFERENTIAL EQUATION

Simulink employs the technic of integration for solving differential equation. It keeps integrating the higher order derivative terms until actual physical quantity is obtained. Following example illustrates the same approach.

EXAMPLE 9.1

To build a Simulink model for solving the following differential equation

$$\frac{d^4 y}{dt^4} + 4\frac{d^3 y}{dt^3} + 2\frac{d^2 y}{dt^2} + 3\frac{dy}{dt} + y(t) = \sin t$$

For input sine wave consider frequency as 4 Hz and run the simulation for 20 seconds.

For modeling it in Simulink, above equation can be rearranged as follows:

$$\frac{d^4 y}{dt^4} = \sin t - 4\frac{d^3 y}{dt^3} - 2\frac{d^2 y}{dt^2} - 3\frac{dy}{dt} - y(t)$$

We know very well that

$$\frac{d^3 y}{dt^3} = \int \frac{d^4 y}{dt^4}, \quad \frac{d^2 y}{dt^2} = \int \frac{d^3 y}{dt^3}, \quad \frac{dy}{dt} = \int \frac{d^2 y}{dt^2} \text{ and } y = \int \frac{dy}{dt}$$

Simulink model is built implementing above mentioned relation using **integrator** block as shown in Figure 9.1.

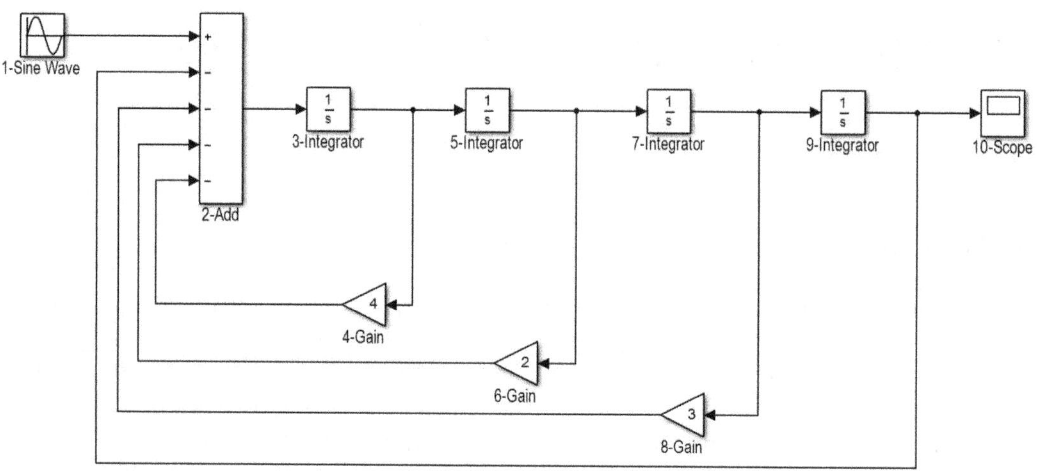

Figure 9.1 Simulink model for solution of differential equation

Details of blocks are given in Table 9.1.

Table 9.1 Details of blocks - Solution of differential equation

Name of block in model	Name of block in Simulink library	Source	Properties
1-Sine wave	Sine wave	Sources	Frequency:8*pi
2-Add	Add	Math operations	List of signs: +----
3-Integrator	Integrator	Commonly used blocks	----
4-Gain	Gain	Commonly used blocks	Right mouse button, Rotate&flip-Flip block Property-Gain:4
5-Integrator	Integrator	Commonly used blocks	----
6-Gain	Gain	Commonly used blocks	Right mouse button, Rotate&flip-Flip block Property-Gain:2
7-Integrator	Integrator	Commonly used blocks	----
8-Gain	Gain	Commonly used blocks	Right mouse button, Rotate&flip-Flip block Property-Gain:3
9-Integrator	Integrator	Commonly used blocks	----
10-Scope	Scope	Sinks	----

Running the model with simulation time of 20 seconds, double clicking **scope** block and then selecting auto scale option, plot shown in Figure 9.2 will be displayed.

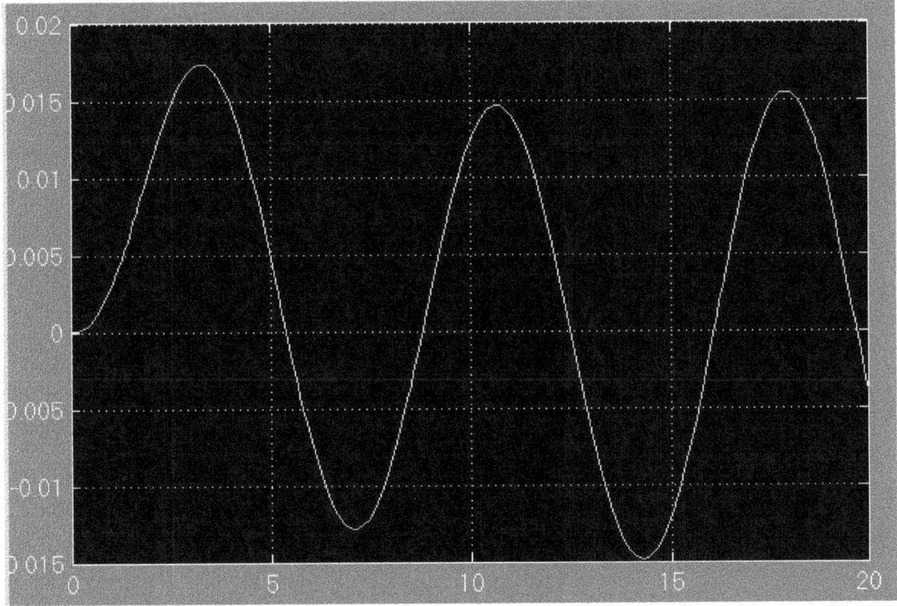

Figure 9.2 Graphical solution for differential equation

Alternative method of solving differential equation is given below.

Let us consider

$$x_1 = y(t)$$

Then

$$x_2 = \frac{dy}{dt}$$
$$x_3 = \frac{d^2y}{dt^2}$$
$$x_4 = \frac{d^3y}{dt^3}$$

From which

$$\dot{x}_1 = x_2 \quad \dot{x}_2 = x_3$$

$$\dot{x}_3 = x_4$$
$$\dot{x}_4 = -x_1 - 3x_2 - 2x_3 - 4x_4 + \sin t$$

Same can be expressed in matrix form as follows.

$$\begin{bmatrix} \dot{x}_1 \\ \dot{x}_2 \\ \dot{x}_3 \\ \dot{x}_4 \end{bmatrix} = \begin{bmatrix} 0 & 1 & 0 & 0 \\ 0 & 0 & 1 & 0 \\ 0 & 0 & 0 & 1 \\ -1 & -3 & -2 & -4 \end{bmatrix} \begin{bmatrix} x_1 \\ x_2 \\ x_3 \\ x_4 \end{bmatrix} + \begin{bmatrix} 0 \\ 0 \\ 0 \\ 1 \end{bmatrix} \sin t$$

Which means

$$\dot{X} = AX + Bu$$

Let us recall

$$x_1 = y(t)$$

Which can be rewritten as

$$Y = \begin{bmatrix} 1 & 0 & 0 & 0 \end{bmatrix} \begin{bmatrix} x_1 \\ x_2 \\ x_3 \\ x_4 \end{bmatrix} + \begin{bmatrix} 0 \end{bmatrix} \sin t$$

Further same can be written as

$$Y = CX + Du$$

From the above equations

$$A = \begin{bmatrix} 0 & 1 & 0 & 0 \\ 0 & 0 & 1 & 0 \\ 0 & 0 & 0 & 1 \\ -1 & -3 & -2 & -4 \end{bmatrix} \quad B = \begin{bmatrix} 0 \\ 0 \\ 0 \\ 1 \end{bmatrix} \quad C = \begin{bmatrix} 1 & 0 & 0 & 0 \end{bmatrix} \quad D = \begin{bmatrix} 0 \end{bmatrix}$$

Same is modeled in Simulink and the associated model is shown in Figure 9.3.

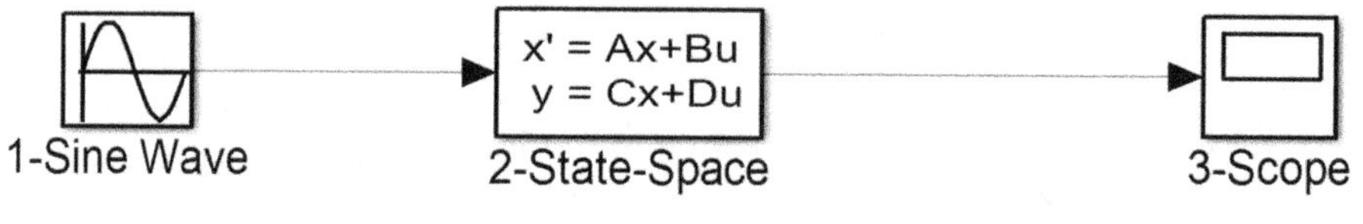

Figure 9.3 Simulink model for solution of differential equation (State-space model)

Details of blocks are given in Table 9.2.

Table 9.2 Details of blocks - Solution of differential equation (State-space model)

Name of block in model	Name of block in Simulink library	Source	Properties
1-Sine wave	Sine wave	Sources	Frequency:8*pi
2-State Space	State-Space	Continuous	A: [0 1 0 0; 0 0 1 0; 0 0 0 1; -1 -3 -2 -4] B:[0 0 0 1]' C:[1 0 0 0] D: [0] Initial conditions: [0 0 0 0]'
3-Scope	Scope	Sinks	----

Running the model with simulation time of 20 seconds, double clicking **scope** block and then selecting auto scale option, plot shown in Figure 9.4 will be displayed.

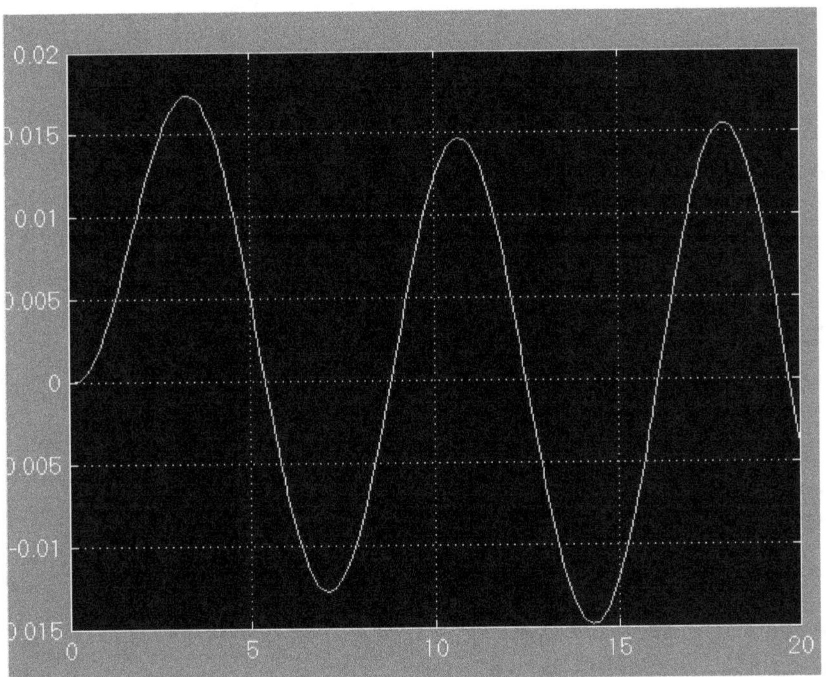

Figure 9.4 Graphical solution for differential equation (State-space model)

It is evident that the results obtained using conventional Simulink modeling approach and state-space model are identical.

9.2 LAPLACE TRANSFORM APPROACH FOR SOLVING DIFFERENTIAL EQUATION

Simulink also enables user to employ an alternative technic to solve a differential equation through Laplace transform approach. Associated example is given below.

EXAMPLE 9.2

To build a Simulink model for solving the following differential equation in Laplace domain

$$m\ddot{x} + c\dot{x} + kx = F_0 \sin \omega t$$

Response for this system in Laplace domain can be expressed as follows:

$$x(s) = \frac{F(s)}{ms^2 + cs + k}$$

Substituting all values

$$x(s) = \frac{50}{10s^2 + 200s + 100} = \frac{1}{0.2s^2 + 4s + 2}$$

Simulink model is shown in Figure 9.5.

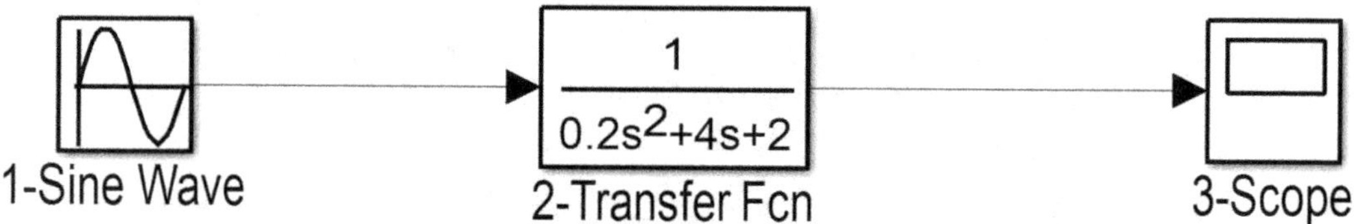

Figure 9.5 Simulink model for response in Laplace domain

Details of blocks are given in Table 9.3.

Table 9.3 Details of blocks - Response in Laplace domain

Name of block in model	Name of block in Simulink library	Source	Properties
1-Sine wave	Sine wave	Sources	Frequency: 6.346 Phase: 1.4528
2-Transfer Fcn	Transfer Fcn	Continuous	Denominator coefficients: [0.2 4 2]
3-Scope	Scope	Sinks	----

Running the model with simulation time of 20 seconds, double clicking **scope** block and then selecting auto scale option, plot shown in Figure 9.6 will be displayed.

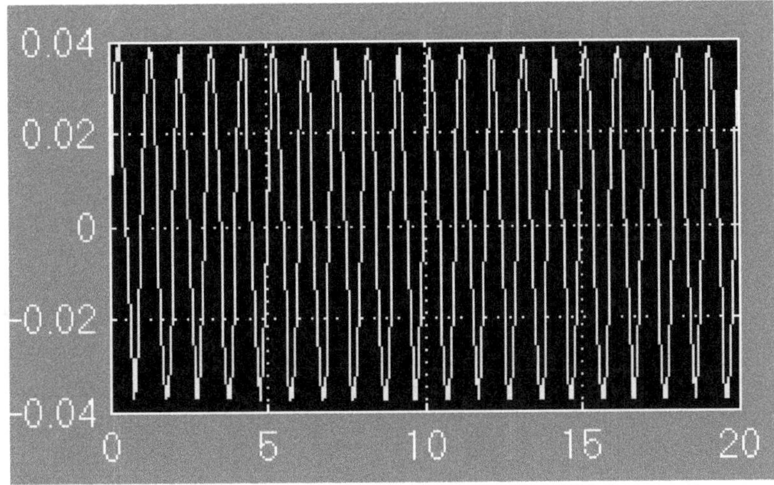

Figure 9.6 Graphical solution for response (Transfer Function model)

9.3 SUMMARY

Solving differential equations using integration approach in Simulink is presented. Simulink provides means to obtain the behavior of actual physical quantity directly from differential equation that consists of derivatives of the said physical quantity. An alternative technic of solving differential equation i.e. using Laplace transform approach is also elaborated.

References

1. Akai, T. J., Applied Numerical Methods, John Wiley & Sons, New York, 1994.
2. Borse, G. J., Numerical Methods with MATLAB, PWS Publishing, Boston, MA, 1997.
3. Boyce W.E., Diprima R.C., Elementary Differential Equations and Boundary Value Problems, 7th Edition, John Wiley & Son, Inc, (2003).
4. Bracewell, R., The Fourier Transform and Its Applications, McGraw-Hill, New York, 1986.
5. Braun, M., Differential Equations and Their Applications, Springer-Verlag, New York, 1978.
6. Chapra, S. and R. Canalel., Numerical Methods for Engineers with Software Programming Applications, 4th edn., McGraw-Hill, New York, 2002.
7. Close, C. M., Modeling and Analysis of Dynamic Systems, 3rd edn., John Wiley & Sons, New York, 2002.
8. Fausett, L. V., Numerical Methods—Algorithms and Applications, Prentice-Hall, Upper Saddle River, NJ, 2003.
9. Fishwick, P. A., Simulation Model Design and Execution—Building Digital Worlds, Prentice-Hall, Upper Saddle River, NJ, 1995.
10. Hairer E., Norsett S. P., Wanner G., Solving ordinary differential equations I: Non-stiff problems, 2nd Edition, Berlin: Springer Verlag, ISBN 978-3-540-56670-0, (1993).
11. Mattheij, R.M.M., and Molenaar, J., Ordinary Differential Equations in Theory and Practice. SIAM Classics in Applied Mathematics 43, SIAM, Philadelphia, PA (2002)
12. Mesterton-Gibbons, M., A Concrete Approach to Mathematical Modeling, Addison-Wesley, Redwood City, CA, 1988.
13. Ralston, A. and H. S. Wilf., Mathematical Methods for Digital Computers, John Wiley & Sons, New York, 1965.
14. Rao, S. S., Applied Numerical Methods for Engineers and Scientists, Prentice-Hall, Upper Saddle River, NJ, 2002.
15. Shampine, L.F., Gladwell, I., and Thompson, S.: Solving ODEs with MATLAB. Cambridge University Press, Cambridge, UK (2003)
16. Smith, W. A., Elementary Numerical Analysis, Prentice-Hall, Englewood Cliffs, NJ, 1986.

17. Smith, J. M., Mathematical Modeling and Digital Simulation for Engineers and Scientists, 2nd edn., John Wiley & Sons, New York, 1987.

18. Stoer, J., and Bulirsch, R., Introduction to Numerical Analysis. Springer-Verlag, New York (2002)

19. Tse, I. E., F. S. Hinkle, and R. T. Marse., Mechanical Vibrations: Theory and Applications, Allyn and Bacon, 1963.

20. Wellstead, P. E., Introduction to Physical System Modelling, Academic Press, London, U.K., 1979.

21. www.mathworks.com